Taonga Pūoro

SINGING TREASURES

Nā roto atu o te pukapuka nei, kua tikina atu ngā ringa rehe o Hirini Melbourne hei hanga anō i ngā taonga pūoro e whakahau ana i ngā reo o ngā atua kia waiata mai anō. Kua roa e hāngū ana nā reira, ko te kauwaka tēnei hei whakatangi anō i a rātou kia unuhia ai te kura huna.

Through this book, the skilled hands of Hirini Melbourne are being utilised to create taonga pūoro and thus are prevailing on the gods to sing once more. They have long been silent, and this book is the medium whereby the gods are invited to make their voices enchant the listeners and to release their unique treasures to inspire people.

Wharehuia Milroy

TAONGA PŪORO

SINGING TREASURES

The musical instruments of the Māori

BRIAN FLINTOFF

CRAIG
POTTON
PUBLISHING

All unacknowledged carving and photographs in *Taonga Pūoro* are the work of the author Brian Flintoff.

First published in 2004 by Craig Potton Publishing
98 Vickerman Street, PO Box 555, Nelson, New Zealand
www.craigpotton.co.nz

Reprinted 2005, 2006

ISBN 1-877333-14-X

Design by Lisa Noble
Printed in China by Everbest Printing Co. Ltd

Contents

Preface

The Haumanu logo depicts a kōkako being drawn to the sound of a nguru.

Haumanu is a loose-knit group of dedicated Māori music players and instrument makers which developed under the leadership of well-known composer and player, the late Dr Hirini Melbourne (1950-2003). Hirini's interest in traditional instruments had initially been stirred by looking at old examples lying silent in their museum cases. He mused sadly on their loneliness. What were the sounds they created? What stories were told about them? And would their music be heard by the coming generations? He set about finding the answers to these questions and subsequently drew together a number of people who were already working on their revival, and others who also wished these treasures would sing again and were prepared to do something about it.

Haumanu had its beginnings at an informal weekend near the top of Pikikiruna on Takaka Hill, near Nelson. When Hirini and I travelled there initially to dedicate a pūtōrino carved from a 35,000-year-old tōtara tree it was early in the day and mist wafted from the mysterious holes scattered throughout the vast expanses of warming marble. He began playing softly, slowly building momentum, and as he played the sound filled the still air above us. Soon the echoes were circling over us and in that magic moment it was as if we were inside a crystal glass singing to the finger's touch. We called that great marble rock nestled in bush Ōhaka Tapu, the Sacred Nest. Several members of the group have returned at other times to film and record at this special place and at the same time we have revived our energies in its special aura.

The name Haumanu can be literally translated as 'breath of birds' and was chosen because of the importance of bird songs in the traditions of the music. The word also means revival and this is the aim of the group. The Haumanu logo depicts our greatest songbird, the kōkako, being attracted by the sound of a flute.

Dr Hirini Melbourne with his pūkāea **Tamanui.**

University of Waikato

One of the plant-filled holes in the great marble rock, **Ōhaka Tapu.**

Craig Potton

The nucleus of Haumanu combined the complementary skills of Hirini, as a musician and composer, with an established status in both Māori and academic circles; Richard Nunns, as an accomplished flute player and multiskilled presenter; and myself as a craftsperson to make replicas of those treasures held safe in the museums. From a hui initiated in 1991 Hirini also drew together such people as Mauri Tirikātene, Rangiiria Hedley, Tūpari Te Whata, Clem Mellish, Ranginui Keefe and Tēpora Kūpenga, John Collins, Te Wārena Taua and Rewi Spragon, all with different areas of expertise but whose intention was to create a human resource that would foster the revival of the instruments. From these initial beginnings the Haumanu 'flock' began to increase over time and those who have joined the ranks are Te Aue Davis, Joe Malcolm, Hemi te Wano, Rangi Kipa, Bernard Makaore, Pōtaka Taite, Aroha Yates-Smith, Warren Warbrick, Moana Maniapoto, Horomona Horo, Robin Slow, James Rickard and James Webster.

Many demonstrations and workshops have been conducted, mostly on marae throughout the country. A collection of instruments constructed at one of the workshops or hui of instrument makers held at Otātara in 1995 was lodged at Te

Papa for future students to have access to. Ngāwara Gordon at the Hei Tiki Gallery in Rotorua has continued the momentum of these hui for makers and players.

Richard Nunns has collated the results of the comprehensive research he and Hirini undertook with elders and other informants over many years, and has compiled this into a major work for which Hirini had begun a parallel Māori version. This is still in production. Richard's readiness to journey out to my workshop with new information to guide my reconstructions, and also to test play the many modifications and variations, is still a vital element in the success of our work.

For several years Hirini, Richard and I have been working towards a smaller publication to supplement our verbal and musical presentations. We wished to provide a reference for those who wanted to continue their interest in both playing and making Taonga Pūoro, these Singing Treasures. Late in 2002, after Hirini was diagnosed with cancer, he gave me the task of compiling this small, long-planned book, saying with his ever-present chuckle, 'I've got a great idea. And the best thing is I just do the idea bit and you do all the work.' This of course makes light of his years of devotion to the journey that brought us to the place where a coherent narrative is possible. This book summarises historical observations and contemporary research by Hirini, Richard, myself and others, and includes translations of Hirini's writings and oral communications. In most cases topics are complemented with some of his songs and, where possible, his own brief interpretations of them. Fortunately Hirini and I were able to complete the outline and share most of the content before he left us. *Taonga Pūoro, Singing Treasures* is therefore presented as a tribute to Hirini.

The readiness of a great number of people to freely provide assistance has been a heart-warming tribute to Hirini's standing and I am very appreciative of it all, especially the inspirational photographs taken by Terry O'Connor who passed away just before this book went to print. I note with gratitude the special contributions of Professor Wharehuia Milroy, Jan Melbourne, Pania Melbourne, Rangiiria Hedley, Richard Nunns, Derek Lardelli, Aroha Yates-Smith, Kiri Bramley, Dr Amiria Henare, Maureen Lander, Awhina Tamarapa and the others at Te Papa, Alan Thomas, Michael Keith, Keith Hill and Tim Gummer at Rattle Records, Jo Paku, Cherie and John Woffindin, Maggie Atkinson, Bob Bickerton, Robbie Burton and the team at Craig Potton Publishing who have turned the concept into a reality, and my wife Julia, for her support and encouragement.

A third dimension has been added to the words and pictures of this book with the inclusion of a sampler CD of Māori music. This has been made possible by the support of the recording companies and the musicians who have kindly given permission to use extracts from their compilations, all of which are highly recommended. It adds the sounds that were absent when Hirini looked into those silent museum cases. A multi-dimensional look at the taonga is available on the DVD that accompanies the CD *Te Hekenga ā Rangi.*[1]

Hirini wished primarily to share this knowledge with his people of Ngai Tūhoe and other Māori, but he also recognised a similarity of human spirit in others and wanted everyone to respectfully share the gifts of his ancestors.

Kia pōkai ake ra i te takapau tuwhara o te pō Kia whiti mai anō te rā Whiti Whiti Whiti mai te rā.	The blankets of night are rolled away The sun shines again. +

Julia Flintoff

On their way to **Ōhaka Tapu** are Haumanu members Brian Flintoff, Richard Nunns and Clem Mellish on the left, with Hirini Melbourne on the right and the crew of Rangiātea Films in the centre.

Note: Hirini's wonderful songs, which appear throughout the book, have also been recorded, sometimes on more than one CD. Hirini was creative and seldom sang his songs the same way each time he recorded them, and was also happy to reuse his material. The symbols at the end of each song show which CD or CDs contain recordings of that song. Full details of the CDs are given in the references at the end of the book.

- * Hirini Melbourne, *Te Wharekura 41*, Learning Media Ltd, Wellington, 1994.
- @ Hirini Melbourne, *Toiapiapi* (book and accompanying tape), Shearwater Associates Ltd, Wellington, 1991.
- \+ Hirini Melbourne & Richard Nunns, *Te Kū Te Whe* (CD with notes), Rattle RAT-D004, 1994.
- \# Hirini Melbourne, *Te Kuraroa*, Kia Ata Mai Educational Trust, 1998.
- ^ Hirini Melbourne, Richard Nunns & Aroha Yates-Smith, *Te Hekenga ā Rangi* (CD and DVD), Rattle RAT DV010, 2003.

INTRODUCTION

In 1849 Matiaha Tiramorehu related the creation story in which Māori music traditions are founded. He gave a genealogy of creation that begins: 'Kei a te Pō te timatatanga o te waiatatanga mai a te Atua. Ko te Ao, ko te Ao mārama, ko te Ao tūroa.' This has been interpreted as 'It was in the night, that the Gods sang the world into existence. From the world of light, into the world of music.'[2]

Creation began in Te Kore, the Void, after the two opposite but complementary elements, Hani (the Seeker) and Puna (the Well Spring), came together at the Sacred Altar. Then followed aeons of generations of Te Pō, the Darkness, which were matched by generations of Te Ao, the Light.

From the ages of Te Ao came our world's primal Sky Father, Ranginui e tū iho nei. From Te Pō came Papatūāuenuku, the Earth Mother. Their names are often abbreviated to Rangi and Papa. Both had families through earlier relationships, and several children of these stayed with Rangi and Papa and are commonly known as their children. This extended family gave us most of the departmental gods of the Māori. The ones met in this book include Tānemahuta, the great procreator and God of the Forests, as well as birds; Tāwhirimātea, the God of the Winds; Whiro, feared as the one responsible for bad deeds and sickness; Tū Matauenga, the fierce God of War; and Rūaumoko, the unborn child who gets restless at times and moves within Papa, creating earthquakes.

All the different types of Māori song stem from the emotions displayed by the gods during the creation aeons. There are songs of sorrow, anger and lament; of loneliness, desire and joy; of peace and love. The voices of the instruments and the movements of dance support and embellish the songs.

Te Wehenga A print depicting Rangi and Papa, with traditional symbols representing some of their children between them.

Māori traditions include a wide range of musical instruments and these are presented here in their family groups, mostly illustrated by contemporary examples that have been used in the revival journey. Because these Taonga Pūoro, singing treasures, can be best appreciated and understood when the cosmogony that guided their creation is known, this book summarises some of the myths and legends that directly relate to them. They are arranged in order of the validating myth that introduces them and authenticates their existence. This sequence fittingly keeps them between the primal parents, Rangi and Papa. These stories have been pieced together from various sources and there are several tribal variations on them, not all of which are in the public domain. However, their theme is consistent and we trust that where local knowledge does not agree with these versions it will be understood that we acknowledge, respect and treasure those variations.

In the following chapters you will learn a little more about the Māori gods associated with Taonga Pūoro. Tunes are named after the Sky Father Rangi, and rhythms come from the heartbeats of Papa, the Earth Mother. Their descendants brought us the instruments to join rhythm and tune. Tānemahuta, the God of the Forest and its creatures, gave the trees from which many instruments are made. Hine pū te hue, one of his daughters, became the ancestress of the gourds

This selection of contemporary Taonga Pūoro shows the variety of materials used to make them.

and began by using her own body as a sounding vessel. Another daughter, Hine Raukatauri, loved her flute so much that she chose to live inside it and became the Goddess of Flute Music. Tāwhirimātea, the God of the Winds, gives breath to the spinning instruments. Tangaroa, the Mighty God of the Seas, is father of the fish which give us sea shells, some of which are made into instruments.

While most instruments have these obvious family origins, others however are created by a union of the families of gods, and so could rightly be included in more than one chapter. Understanding these concepts helps to give some insight into the values that are placed on the instruments, the music and the materials they are created from. It also helps in giving respect to the many spiritual aspects of these taonga, which are not part of the public domain and are therefore only alluded to in this book. Taonga Pūoro were also vehicles of entertainment, and this aspect is the focus of the book – however, as we have so often noticed when performing, these instruments also convey a spiritual dimension that transcends the sounds they can create, which is an essential part of appreciating their value.

Today, instrument materials that are endangered, extinct or no longer appropriate are being substituted by newly adopted children of the natural world. For instance, we make bone kōauau from ostrich to replicate the extinct moa, and deer or emu bones are substituted for human bones.

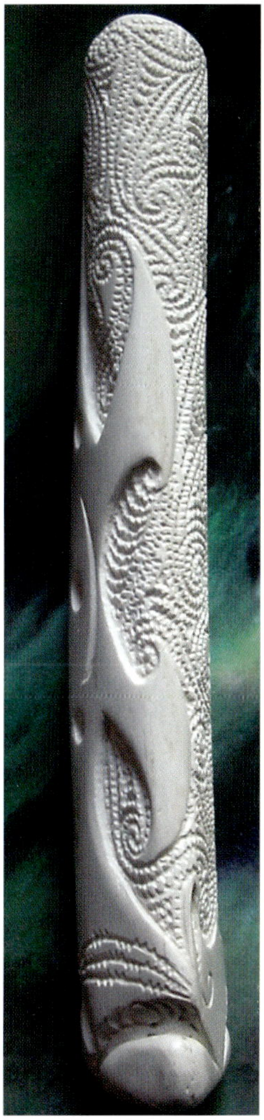

This kōauau is carved from a moa leg bone. It is a carved lizard design inspired by traditional human bone kōauau held in the British Museum.

Te Uira is a 'simple' percussive whalebone pākuru, but playing techniques for this instrument are so complex that many of their intricacies are, for now, lost.

Richard Nunns

Mauri Tirikātene is playing his pūtōrino in the style he was taught as a youth.

The most commonly heard instruments are the flutes and a wide variety of styles are made in a wide range of materials. All instruments are seen as individuals and so naturally have different voices, but these differences are kept within the boundaries of their family's origins. Innovation that crosses these boundaries is strongly discouraged as it could contravene the natural order of things as set down by the gods, and marked by the Pou Tiri Ao, or guardian posts.

Traditionally all tunes were intended to complement words: the instruments were not used just to make musical sounds. There are many references to the words being breathed into the music of a number of the instruments and several legends tell of listeners being given secret messages through their playing. There are many mysteries locked within all these instruments. Along with entertainment their uses in healing, sending messages, opening and closing life's doors and in other significant ceremonies are still practised.

It is important to understand that the Māori did not use a musical scale of semitones or have a set scale. They compressed their scale into microtones of such subtlety that many early Western observers failed to appreciate it. The method of blowing the flutes allows adaptability to adjust the pitch with small movements of the tongue and lips. Therefore it is often unnecessary to create instruments to a set pitch, though attaining an approximate pitch suited to a song is advisable where the flute is accompanying a singer. Several instruments have soft, private voices suitable for playing in the confines of the small whare, or houses. Others have louder voices for use in a large meeting house or even for sending messages outdoors.

In 1807 it was noted that 'every man was his own musician' and with such small and portable instruments 'they were never at a loss for entertainment'.[3] Unfortunately, for a variety of reasons, the use of these traditional instruments declined. Some became children's toys, and some were hidden away or destroyed because they were deemed too precious and special to be denigrated. Some are retained by the families of their owners and others were sold to collectors or given as special taonga to mark momentous events. Sadly, some playing techniques are now lost, even for the 'simple' instruments such as the percussive pākuru.

The greatest decline was probably through the double pressures of, first, missionaries and teachers who discouraged the use of the instruments because they did not understand them (or understood their spiritual nature all too well), and, second, the appeal of newly introduced European instruments. These often even took on traditional names so that a saxophone or clarinet could be called a kōauau.

Because musical instruments were taonga they were well made and thus very collectable. This was strikingly evident when we visited the British Museum in London where they have more pūtōrino in their collection than in all the museums in New Zealand.

Only a handful of old recordings were made, mostly on wax cylinders. The only known later recordings were of Mrs Paeroa Wineera, and a few items from this treasure are available on a CD, *Traditional Music of the Māori*.[4] Careful listening reveals her method of 'singing' the words into her kōauau. These sounds, along with old songs that were known to be used with the instruments, are a valuable guide to the revival process. Even the earliest recordings, however, were of players who had become attuned to the Western musical scale and so are not a true guide to the ancient music. Ancient musicians are known to have taken inspiration from natural sounds; accordingly, these natural sounds and the voices the instruments are able to produce have been important in the revival process.

The 1980s and 1990s saw a revival of the instrumental traditions by a number of individuals, notably Joe Malcolm and Donna Hall. In 1985, under the umbrella of Ngā Puna Waihanga, the Māori Artists and Writers Organisation, the late Ivan Ehau organised the first major workshop on kōauau and pūtōrino making and playing at Te Araroa, with Joe Malcolm as its kaumātua or elder consultant.

Fortunately another kaumātua, Mauri Tirikātene, was present, as he had been taught to play the pūtōrino when a boy in the Whanganui area and was able to pass on his expert guidance. Both Richard Nunns and I were workshop tutors at this wānanga, and this is where we first met Hirini, who was one of those making their first instrument. So began our friendship and partnership.

Since then a great number of wānanga have been held on marae throughout the country. This has led to the collection of a considerable body of new information from many elders throughout Aotearoa who were able to correct and modify what had been gleaned from books and museums, and even bring to light hitherto unrecorded instruments. Interestingly, it was often only after hearing the sounds of the instruments that many old people rediscovered forgotten memories. These pieces of information have been the key to rebuilding the traditions and our sincere thanks go to all those who have shared their knowledge.

Many individuals have retained pockets of knowledge that sometimes resurface when their time is right or are kept precious within trusted family circles awaiting their time. It is always exciting to be able to add these to the basket of Taonga Pūoro knowledge and I look forward to gaining more of these to share with those who wish to learn.

This book uses the most common of a range of names that have been collected for most instruments. They are not comprehensive but are intended as a beginning so that more people can share the entrancing experience and lifelong interest that these singing treasures offer. And, like many of those involved in this revival, they may find their lives much enhanced by their magic.

TAKU PŪTŌRINO

Taku Pūtōrino
Nō wai rā ngā ngutu
Hai whakapā ki ōu
hai puhi i te hauora
kia rangonahia ai anō tō reo?

Kai te rongo mai koe
E Hineraukatauri
Te puhi o te tangi
Hotuhotu mokemoke
O ngā mōteatea.

Raukatauri,
Whose breath
could bring you life
And make you sing again?

Hirini Melbourne* @

Hirini Melbourne playing a double pūtōrino named **Amokura**, which was made to hold the amokura feather between its two surrounding chambers.

1

Rangi
THE TUNES

The setting sun silhouettes the skyline from Tāhunanui, Nelson. The patterning of the clouds and the sea, and the shape of the skyline can all suggest new songs.

Craig Potton

Dr Ferry Boehme

A bubbling stream sings its way down a mountain near the Mt Angelus hut in Nelson Lakes National Park.

Shaun Barnett/Black Robin Photography

Kōkako is the blue-wattled crow. Its pure song amplifies the sound of Raukatauri, goddess of flute music.

Rangi is the term applied to all tunes, and it is also the shortened name of the Sky Father, Ranginui e tū iho nei, in whose realm they exist, from whom they are descended and to whom they ascend. Just as the universe took its physical shaping from the singing of the gods, music can be perceived as creating shapes in the silence. With this concept as an anchor, we too can strive to create music that makes pleasing shapes in the same way that carvers or other artists do in the physical world.

For earlier generations music was so special that it needed a reason and an occasion to be played. It was not customary to make melodies that stood alone. The music of kōauau and pūtōrino always had words and an expert player could make these heard through the instrument.

Those early musicians' use of microtone scales had the effect of compressing a normal number of notes into the range of just a few notes in the modern scale.

As the instruments were made to complement the singing they are an obvious anchor stone for development of musical ideas within those traditional parameters. Traditional music reflects natural sounds and, like the language, its intonation conveys a mood that is then complemented by the words. Therefore, capturing the right sound pattern is essential to creating a song. For inspiration we can listen to the sounds around us, so take time and listen to the sounds of wind in the trees or whistling against a sharp corner, surf crashing onto rocks or swishing up and down the gravel on the beach, a lake's waves lapping against the bank, the timeless inspiration of bubbling streams, thermal bubbles and gurgles. In listening you will learn to focus your hearing, just as you focus your eyes in looking.

The wonderful songs of kōkako, tūi and korimako (bellbirds) are phrased as waiata, sometimes even with choruses. Each bird's song also carries its own message and careful listening will allow you to appreciate the male tūi's kōroki, or loud call of welcome to the new day. This is subtly different from the softer korihi of the female tūi.

Bird songs also provide a lesson in adaptation. They are adapted to today's sound world but the adaptations are done in a way that retains the songs' original character. For instance, the tūi will intertwine the song of a chaffinch and other sounds into its verses and kōkako have even been heard to copy the sound of a chainsaw or a barking deer. Sometimes, when a tauhou or waxeye is alone it stops its twittering flocking calls and 'whispers' an enchanting series of ever-changing verses. This is a personal song and an inspiration to any composer. The lilting song of the riroriro or grey warbler has a beautiful flowing sound that keeps within a limited range of notes. It does not attempt to sing above the noise of wind and rain

Raukatauri, the casemoth, is the personification of the goddess of the same name, who loved her flute so much that she chose to live inside it. She is pictured here by the flowers of the kōwhai tree.

Far right: An evening song is echoed by the reflection of Mt Angelus in Lake Angelus.

but on calm days its trilling voice carries messages of the bounty in Tāne's forest and reminds us of the interdependence of all its varied parts.

Then there are the quiet sounds of some insects. I have talked to only one person who has listened to the casemoth, Raukatauri, the shy Goddess of Flute Music, but that tiny sound inspires the kōkako's beautiful song, as is explained in a story to be told later. Noisy cicada songs also have a special place in tradition. There are several families of these insects and each has its own unique song. These are isolated on *Karanga Voices, Volume 4*.

You can also look around you at the music described by the undulations of a section of the skyline as it rises and falls, the shape of a rock, a pattern in weaving or painting with its changing textures or colours, the shapes of a leaf edge or the hanging fern, Ngā Makawe a Raukatauri, which would be an inspirational theme for both words and tune. Even the ethereal colour patterns of a rainbow and their reversal in the double bow that comprises the complementary male and female elements can become our inspiration.

A recommended place to start learning about Māori music is by listening to early recordings of songs such as those on the CDs accompanying the book *He Waiata Onamata,*[5] which also features instrumental sounds. The music on the CDs referred to throughout this book, some of which is included on the sampler CD that accompanies it, has proved to be a very successful learning tool for some players. Rangi Dewes's LP *Mōteatea* is hard to get now but invaluable. However, even early recordings like this were already influenced by contact with European music, so going back to nature is one way of returning to the sounds that influenced the early musicians.

Karanga Voices, Volume 4, a recent CD recording by the Asia Pacific Archive, School of Music, Victoria University,[6] has an interesting collection of bird and insect songs for those who find it hard to access and identify these sounds. *Pūkaha, Songs from the Forest*, a fundraising CD from the National Wildlife Centre Trust at Mount Bruce in Masterton,[7] contains a wealth of inspirational birdsong. The accompanying booklet with supporting songs by Rangitaane o Wairarapa is full of valuable information about the birds on the recording.

A Song of the Winds and Waters

He hau mihi	Greet the wind
He hau pai e	Praise the wind
Tuku ora ki te rangi e	that brings breath
Hei hauora mō te ao	for the world
Hau manu, hau miri	Winds of affection
Hau kāinga, hau ora.	Winds of life.
Te wai rere	Flowing water
He wai mata	of tears
Tuku ora ki te whenua	Bringing life
Hei waiū mō te ao	to the earth
Waipuna, waihanga	Releasing song
Waiata, wairua.	Reviving spirit.

Hirini Melbourne @

2

Hine Pū Te Hue

THE GOURDS

The exquisite kōwhaiwhai design covering this hue or gourd, which has been named **Mau te Aroha**, was painted by Heeni Kerekere.

In southern myth Tangaroa was the first husband of Papa, the Earth Mother. He returned from a long absence to find that Papa was now the partner of Rangi. They fought a great battle for her affections until Rangi was speared through both legs by the jealous Tangaroa. Deciding that honour was now satisfied, he spared the life of his nephew Rangi and left the pair.

The injuries to Rangi had forced the two primal parents, Papa, the Earth Mother, and Rangi, the Sky Father, into an eternal embrace. Eventually the children of Rangi and Papa, who were also gods, became dissatisfied with the continual darkness and the confined space of the world between their parents. They argued about separating them to allow life to flourish in a more spacious world.

Some attempted the task but it was eventually accomplished by Tāne, who lay on his back and used his mighty legs to push Rangi aloft. There was an horrendous upheaval at this great change and the sadness of Rangi and Papa at their separation is still manifested by the tears of love that drop from Rangi as rain, and the misty sighs of love that rise from Papa.

The divisions and anger between the dissenting children spilled over into fighting, until one of the children of Tānemahuta and Hinerauāmoa, Hine pū te hue, took the wrath of the gods into herself and gave out peace. There are still outbreaks of violence, as we know too well when Rūaumoko stirs within Papa and the earth shakes, or the winds of Tāwhirimātea tear down some of Tāne's trees, but things are much quieter because of her intervention.

Hine pū te hue became the mother of the gourd family. Traditionally most gourds, or hue, were used for the humble task of storing food. Conversely, some remained special and were used as containers for invocations or prayers which could then be kept safe for quick release in times of need. Other hue were used to make music.

All the musical instruments made from hue are like their ancestress and sing songs that are peaceful and calming to the human soul. Through them, we too can tell Hine pū te hue our troubles and our secrets which she will keep safe and then calm us with her beautiful, peaceful sounds.

Poi Āwhiowhio

Musical instruments made from gourds include the poi āwhiowhio or whistling gourd. As these instruments recreate the spirit voices of the winds they are sometimes seen as members of their other family, the wind family. Their songs are used to send invocations to Tānemahuta to seek his blessing on the season for catching his children, the birds. They are also used as song catchers: the rhythmical whistlings of a poi āwhiowhio can become the stimulus for joining ideas and sound into song.

Poi āwhiowhio are medium-sized gourds which are swung on a cord that can be threaded through a hole in the neck or even through neck and base. They have from one to three holes in the sides at the widest part, and through these the seeds can be removed. They can also be ornamented with feathers, though care must be taken or the sound will be impaired. As they rotate they make a chattering whistle. Some sound a bit like the song of a flock of tauhou or waxeyes; others like a riroriro or warbler; and some like the elusive mātātā or fernbird; but in all cases the poi āwhiowhio has a very quiet song that needs concentration to appreciate it.

To Hirini's great surprise, when he and Richard were playing poi āwhiowhio to a school group one day the sound stirred one child to great excitement. Later it was explained that the pupil was profoundly deaf but could actually hear something at last. This wonderfully satisfying moment is typical of certain lucky people's experience when a particular instrument seems to choose them.

Terry O'Connor

Poi Pū This poi āwhiowhio, with its tassel of pūkeko feathers, whispers a bird-like twittering when swung around on its cord.

A Spirit Song for the Birds

Poi āwhiowhio	Whirling twirling poi
Āmiorangi	Circling in the air
E kō nei i te wao nui tapu a Tāne	Proclaiming the sanctuary of Tāne
He reo wairua	You are the spirit voice of the birds.
Nō ngā manu e.	

Hirini Melbourne* +

Hopurangi

Hopurangi are a recent innovation, and resemble a miniature poi āwhiowhio. Made of bone or wood, they are not gourds, but twitter in the same way and seek to remind us of the power of Hine pū te hue as a peacegiver. They can also be worn as a pendant to provide a handy 'rubbish bin' for troubles, then swung to whisper a soothing song of peace. The hopurangi is included as an example of innovation that keeps within the traditions and seeks to retain them by using them in the everyday world. As the name indicates, these tiny gems are also song catchers: the sounds, which vary with the speed of their twirl, can suggest the essence of a song to a keen listener.

These instruments were originally inspired by a pendant carved from a kamani seed pod worn by Hawaiian artist Sam Kaai. He used it as his song accompaniment when I met him after a series of Taonga Pūoro workshops in Hawaii. When I later adapted the idea to work in bone he was delighted, and passed on that his instrument, called matangi, was used by the coastal people of Hawaii to summon the wind when at sea, while inland people used it to call birds in the forest, just as Māori used the poi āwhiowhio.

Ororuarangi

Ororuarangi are long flutes similar to a pūtōrino. They are remembered as being made from the long neck of a gourd with just two finger holes (wenewene) side by side in the centre. Their name echoes a remembered ability to jump between two sound pitches. Tōroa wing bone examples have been collected from Rekohu, the Chatham Islands, and also in the north of Aotearoa. Some have been found with these finger holes joined together to make a mouth-like shape and one also has a 3 mm hole on the underside. Trials with other materials such as ostrich and deer leg bones have produced passable replicas.

Terry O'Connor

These miniature song catchers are hopurangi, an innovation that retains a tradition and makes it available in a wearable form.

These ororuarangi are replicas; **Kakeroa** (top) is made from the neck of a hue and **Rerekohu** from the wing bone of an albatross.

A Song for the Ororuarangi

Whakarongo	Listen
Ki te reo āio	to the calming sounds of Hine pū te hue
O Hine pū te hue	Which the ororuarangi's song
E ororuarangi nei	offers the world.
Ki te ao.	

Hirini Melbourne*

Kōauau Ponga Ihu

Kōauau ponga ihu are tiny gourds with the neck removed. The name translates as a 'flute played with the nostril', and played that way these simple instruments create my very favourite sounds. Their sweet, soft music can mesmerise a large audience with no need for amplification. I remember an occasion when Richard followed the performance of a well-amplified band in Kimiora auditorium at Turangawaewae. He stepped away from the microphones with only this insignificant instrument cupped in his hands, yet he was able to completely captivate the audience.

The best sounds seem to come from gourds about 65–90 mm high, but not all small gourds like to sing and those with reasonably thick walls are best. I did coax one reluctant gourd to sing by fitting an insert which reduced the neck size to 10 mm, but it plays only with the breath of the nose. Two finger holes of around 2–2.5 mm are drilled into the wide section of the body at places best decided on by holding the instrument in two hands as if playing. With the index finger of the right hand blocking one nostril, the next finger can manipulate one hole, and the left index finger can operate the other, so holes are put where the fingers comfortably rest.

Breath of Mine

Hau ki tua	Breath from beyond
Hau ki waho	Breath from without
Hau ki roto i ahau nei	Breath from within
Hei kawe rangi	Become the melody
Mō te kupu e.	For my thoughts and words.

Hirini Melbourne* +

The simplicity of this tiny kōauau ponga ihu belies the rich and enchanting songs it can create.

The beautiful fitted cloak on this hue rarā, named **Hoki mai i te Aroha** was woven in place by Veranora Puketapu-Hetet.

Hue Rarā

Hue rarā are shakers, and the seeds of the gourd are removed and replaced with small stones to create a strong rhythm. A carved stopper provides the finishing touch. These are rhythmic instruments which also belong in the family of Papa, but because their sound is mellowed in the characteristic way of the gourds, they are introduced here with their birth mother.

Hue Puruwai

Hue puruwai are also shakers, medium-sized gourds with their seeds intact. When shaken, they create the soothing sounds of a bubbling stream.

A Lament from Hue Puruwai

Māringiringi	Spill forth
Māturuturu	Trickle forth
Te ua	Pour forth
Roimata e.	Teardrops of love.

Hirini Melbourne*

Hue Puruhau

Hue puruhau are large dried gourds with the seeds removed. No finger holes are drilled, but the top is cut off leaving a neck, which when blown over creates a vibrant bass sound. This sound emulates that of the booming of a male kākāpō as it sends its message over a large area to impress a prospective mate with its night song.

A Song of Kākāpō

Kākāpō, Kākāpō	In the dark
Manu kura huna o te pō	of night
Kākāpō, Kākāpō	Kākāpō
Manu kura huna o te pō	sends booming
Whakarongo rā	sounds of hope
Ki te pahū	and desperate entreaty.
O te poho	
O te Kākāpō	In the dark
Kākāpō, Kākāpō	of night
E karanga nei	Kākāpō booms.
Kia whai hoa ai	
Mo te pō roa e	
Kākāpō, Kākāpō	
Manu kura huna o te pō.	

Hirini Melbourne @ #

The sound of a stream bubbling its way over rocks is evoked when this hue puruwai is shaken.

Hue puruhau emulate the booming bass notes of a male kākāpō.

3

Tāne

FATHER OF MANY SONGMAKERS

This exquisite nguru, with eyes and fingerholes inlaid with paua shell and its flax cord tied to a bore-cleaning muka poi, is part of the collection of the Museum of New Zealand Te Papa Tongarewa (Ref. No. OL000021).

The beauty of the pounamu complemented by Clem Mellish's masterful crafting makes this karanga manu an attractive and useful ethnic pendant.

Tānemahuta, one of the children of Rangi and Papa, was responsible for first separating his parents. He then assumed the task of clothing them in beauty as befitted their great status. To make a marvellous night cloak for Rangi he took the peaceful tribe of Tama Rēreti up to the heavens in their waka, the canoe Uruao. There they were given immortality as a reward for their conduct and they still adorn the night sky wonderfully. At night we can see their waka Uruao anchored up there. It is also known as the constellation Scorpio and it can be located by following the line of the anchor rope, the Pointers. These point the other way to the anchor stone, which we know as Mahutonga, the Southern Cross.

Tāne then worked to clothe Papa. He mated with a number of female deities who produced all the different varieties of plants and trees. He was not pleased, however, when the plants began moving around and ruining his design so he was forced to secure them by putting them upside down so that their hair became rooted in the ground and their limbs waved in the wind. He continued mating with other female deities to produce the birds which add colour and sound to his creation.

With no predatory mammals, primal Aotearoa was a kingdom of birds, many of them singers whose dawn and evening choruses still leave an indelible impression on most listeners. The bodies for many of the other instrument families come from the tree children of Tāne, whose wood and leaves are used to produce a large variety of sounds.

SONGS OF THE BIRDS

Karanga Manu

Karanga manu or kōauau pūtangitangi are calling flutes. The bird calls they imitate were brought back to life when Richard found a flute carved from stone in the collection of the then Dominion Museum of New Zealand, now Te Papa Tongarewa. It was a slender piece of stone with a cupped hole in one end. Later the use of these instruments was verified by Mauri Tirikātene when talking with stone carver Clem Mellish. He said, 'originally, the purpose of these tiny flutes was to lure birds by mimicking their own calls, sometimes to bring them into the hunter's range for easy capture. By placing the pursed lips at the correct angle to the mouthpiece, the player is able to mimic several kinds of bird calls. As an added attraction a karanga manu can be worn as a very special ethnic pendant.' Today these little flutes can create interesting and humorous responses from garden birds and forest dwellers alike, and inspired by these beautiful sounds you can create your own bird songs.

Karanga Weka

In the Hall of Mankind at the British Museum lies a small soapstone carving shaped like a nguru but with only the one finger hole at its upturned end. It was a great surprise when I put this to my lips and heard the distinctive bird call of the weka, a cheeky echo far from home. Replicas of that lone remnant have since revealed that karanga weka can also be played as melodic instruments or used to add the weka's vocal colour to a song like the one below.

That original karanga weka is 55 mm long with a bore tapering steeply in from 23 mm. It has just one 8 mm finger hole tapering inward from the upturn. By flicking the finger off this hole while blowing, the call of the weka is produced. To communicate with weka the dimensions may need to be changed to suit local conditions as trials show that these birds have dialects that require different pitches of instruments in order to elicit a response.

A Song About the Cheeky Weka

Karanga wekaweka
Karanga wekaweka
Wekaweka whakatoi
Wekaweka whakatoi
Wekaweka hīkoi
Poutoti toitoi
Timotimo toro haere e.

Cheeky weka
Cocky weka
Wacky weka
Strutting on stilts.

Hirini Melbourne* @

Tuarōria

Tuarōria are leaves folded and blown through to become singing leaves. Their primary use may have been to imitate bird calls in order to attract them closer. However, since bird songs are an integral part of the origins of the Taonga Pūoro repertoire, the sounds of the tuarōria are an appropriate embellishment.

Karamu or taupata leaves (both coprosma species) are widely available and good to use but it is worthwhile trying others to find your own favourites. Gently fold around the centre rib. Hold near the stem end between one thumb and finger and near the other end with the other thumb and a finger. This will create a tunnel by the stem to blow into and also allow you to vary the tension at the sounding lips of the leaf's sides which then alters the pitch.

Some waxy-surfaced leaves with parallel veins, such as harakeke (flax), turutu (inkberry) or libertia, can be made to sing by drawing them between the fingers as demonstrated by Richard Nunns on the CD *Karanga Voices*.

Te Mōrehu is a soapstone replica of the only known karanga weka, which is held in the British Museum, London.

The shiny coprosma leaves are ideal to use as tuarōria and imitate a number of different bird calls.

A Song of the Birds' Dawn Chorus

E kō, e kō	Sing! Resound!
Ngā manu e	O ye birds in the garden of Tāne
I roto i te māra a Tāne	
Kia hiki ake ai te atakura	That the shadows of dawn are dispersed
Kia whiti ake ai te rā.	And the warming rays of the sun awaken life.

Hirini Melbourne*

SONGS OF THE INSECTS

In the forests of Tānemahuta when the evening bird song fades to silence, and the noisy orchestra of cicadas end their performance, the gentler chirruping of the crickets and katydids can be heard. Then, as our ears gradually become accustomed to the silence, a new chorus begins. But until the echoing call of ruru, the owl, warns of danger, this chorus is so muted that it is mostly audible only to the myriad night creatures. This is the time of the insects – the casemoth, the weta and all their friends. The tiny songs of these small children of Tāne are acknowledged by a group of instruments that also create quiet songs.

Rōria

These very quiet instruments, which can be likened to a Jew's harp, use a slender tongue of wood or bone which is plucked to create vibrations. These are amplified and modified by manipulation of the player's mouth, which becomes the resonator. They are used to suggest words while being played. Early traders found that the metal Jew's harps, which became more durable substitutes, were in great demand and were avidly examined and even modified to suit Māori players' requirements.

A 100 mm sliver of dry kareao (supplejack), mataī, mānuka, maire or kauwae upoko hue (jawbone of a pilot whale) makes a good instrument. Sometimes this sliver is bound to a holding rod. A wider strip of wood or bone with two slots cut to create a central tongue (see photo) gives an instrument with almost identical characteristics that is easier to learn to play on. The width, length and thickness required to produce the right vibrations of this 'tongue' will vary with different materials, so experimentation is the only way to achieve the desired effect.

Te Huruhuru is a rōria made from the flexible thin area of a pilot whale's jawbone.

Te Kū

Te kū is a bow with a single string which is tapped with either a rod or the knuckles while using the mouth cupped over the string as a modifying resonator, as with the rōria. Bows made from dry kareao (supplejack) are mentioned in the sparse information on this instrument, but thinned down whale rib and other flexible woods have shown acceptable suitability in trials of several sizes from 400 mm up. All work, though dry, springy kareao works best.

No traditional strings have survived so it is worth experimenting with various light cords or nylon fishing gut to find the one that suits your instrument. When stringing a kū, drill a small hole in one end of the bow to pass a knot-ended cord through and cut a slit in the other end which will catch on another knot. This allows easy untensioning of the kū when not in use. It also provides a cord with no hindrances to affect its minute vibrations. A tiny sliver of bamboo or the delicate long flight bone of an albatross wing makes a great striker for a kū.

The most expressive response is achieved by holding the kū so that the cord goes between the partially open lips while being tapped with a light rod or the knuckles or fingers. Varying the bow tension and the mouth and tongue shapes, and using different strikers, creates the captivating song of this quiet instrument. These sounds are brought to life beautifully when amplified in the following song as recorded on *Te Hekenga ā Rangi*.

This kū named **Tāwhana** is made from a length of supplejack, the bush vine. Its striker is an albatross bone, and it is decorated with the wing of a tūi and two pilot whale teeth.

Terry O'Connor

Pao Pao Pao

Pao pao i te aho Kū	Tap, tap the string of the Kū
Aho Kū, aho Kū.	
Tāwhana tāwhana, kōpiko kōpiko.	The long and curving Kū
Pao pao pao pao i te aho Kū	
Pao! Pao! Pao!	
Pao pao i te aho Kū	Strike, strike the string of the Kū
Aho Kū, aho Kū.	
Ngū waruwaru, ngū waruwaru	Stroke, stroke the string of the Kū
Pao pao! Pao pao!	
Pao pao i te aho Kū	Pluck, pluck the string of the Kū
Aho Kū, aho Kū	
Kia mao te ua, kia mao te ua	Pass away the showers
Pao pao i te aho Kū	
Pao pao! Pao pao!	
Pao pao mai i te aho Kū	Strum, strum the string of the Kū
Pao pao! Pao pao!	
E tāwhana nei, e tāwhana nei	See the rainbow appears
Pao pao! Pao pao!	
E ua! E ua!	Let it rain
E mao! E mao!	Let it cease
Te Kū e! Te Kū e!	in the resonant singing
Pao pao i te aho Kū, aho Kū.	of the rhythms of the Kū.

Hirini Melbourne ^

4

Tangaroa

Father of Shell Instruments

This beautifully made and well worn pūtātara with its tassel of pūkeko feathers comes from the Whanganui region. Collection of the Museum of New Zealand Te Papa Tongarewa, Wellington (Ref. No. ME003937).

After the separation of Rangi and Papa, when peace had been restored by Hine pū te hue, the god children of Rangi and Papa realised that they did not have all the understanding they needed to establish the vast new world. They discussed this and sent Tānemahuta to climb to the topmost heaven, Rangiātea, to obtain the required knowledge. The task was difficult and made even harder because Tāne's brother, Whiro, had hoped to be chosen for this task. When rejected he sent his evil hordes of mosquitoes, sandflies and others to try to make Tāne turn back. But Tāne persevered and in that uppermost heaven he received from Io Matua Kore three baskets with their own spheres of knowledge, as well as mauri stones to keep them vital. On his return these kete were used to establish the first whare wānanga or university. To indicate the success of his mission to those waiting below, two pūtātara named Hāururangi and Rangi Whakaaraara were trumpeted.

Tangaroa is the mighty God of the Oceans and the fish are his children with Hine Moana. From the largest of the shellfish we get the pūtātara instruments that are first recorded in this myth.

The calls of these shell instruments parallel those of the seabirds of Tangaroa's realm. They do not sing songs like many land birds but their calls are effective at sending their messages through the noise of wind and waves. In contrast to their strident daytime calls are the night-time murmuring of nesting tītī (Sooty shearwater) recorded on *Karanga Voices*.

Pūtātara

The most commonly heard shell instrument is the pūtātara, or pūmoana, a conch shell trumpet. There are stories of its signalling calls being used to transmit messages and some of these calls have been remembered, so that when an instrument was recently presented on a marae in Tūwharetoa the call used by a returning party well over 200 years earlier was used again as its first song.

Pūtātara were not readily available but stories are told of an approaching party being identified by the sound of the shell they played. Large shells like the triton (*Triton australis*) are not native to Aotearoa, and are only rarely washed up on northern beaches, so the smaller native shells (*Charonia lampas rubicunda*) were mostly used. Some early examples had a wooden insert fitted to a hole made in the side. As this is seen in more than one museum example, it may have been a way of modifying the sound.

Terry O'Connor

Pū Whakaoro is a pūtātara made from a triton shell and adorned with three pīngao kete symbolising the Kete Mātauranga of tradition. These shells rarely wash up on New Zealand beaches, and were so unique that instruments could be identified by their call.

Cambridge University

This pūtātara with its sound-altering muka poi was probably collected by Captain James Cook on his first expedition to New Zealand in 1769–71. It is one of only a few known to have a wooden insert stitched over an opening in its bell. Courtesy of Cambridge University Museum of Archaeology and Anthropology.

Matangi Āwhio A pūpakapaka carved by James Rickard. These long-necked instruments produce a multi-harmonic range of sounds.

Terry O'Connor

A legend from Wharekahika on the East Coast and also from Oaro in the south tells of a strange song that was heard occasionally coming from the depths of the sea. Much speculation arose to explain the phenomenon. Then one day a shell was pulled to the surface clinging to a net and from it came the mystery song. This shell was made into a trumpet and given the name Hinemokemoke, the Lonely Girl, and the singing voice was preserved forever within it.

Although pūtātara were most commonly employed to sound a signalling call or to make an announcement, these instruments can be used in a more melodic way, like Hine Mokemoke, by manipulating the opening with a dampening object like a poi or simply with the hand. Some shells can also be played melodically when cross-blown like a kōauau. A long-stemmed pūtātara is called a pūpakapaka (see illustration).

The conch trumpet is a common instrument throughout the Pacific and beyond but there are few places where a wooden mouthpiece is attached. This combining of shell and wood brings together Tāne and Tangaroa, the mighty Gods of Earth and of Sea Beings. When these are bound together with the leaves of the sand sedge, pīngao, they signify the importance of a peace offering as recalled in the following myth.

Terry O'Connor

This small conch from Farewell Spit is bound to its mouthpiece with the golden leaves of pīngao.

Pīngao had been given by Tāne to Tangaroa to cement peace after the anger caused by the separation of Rangi and Papa. Aeons later, when Pīngao poked out her head at a very low tide, she spied the handsome Kākaho, the plumed flower stalks of the toetoe. As she watched them dancing in the breeze she fell desperately in love. She was so infatuated that she sought Tangaroa's consent to leave the sea and go ashore to be with her beloved Kākaho. Very reluctantly, Tangaroa agreed but warned her of the dangers involved in making the transition.

Pīngao set off excitedly but found that trudging through sand was very difficult for a sea plant. Sadly, when the morning sun rose and the time of the magic release had to end she was only three-quarters of the way up the beach. Her cries for help went unheeded: Kākaho was far too busy admiring himself to even hear her. Tangaroa could not help and Pīngao was fixed in her new place, unable to be with her beloved. She remains there today, kept alive by the tears of Tangaroa as they splash on the shore.

Fortunately the story ends with the lovers united as they are woven together in the tukutuku panels of the wharenui or meeting house. This also becomes the symbolic confirmation for the union of two people.

The art of carving is another gift from Tangaroa, and so the carving of the wooden mouthpiece for a pūtātara is another symbolic act of cementing the peace.

Pūpū Harakeke

For the Ngāti Kuri people of the Far North the song of the pūpū harakeke, or flax snails, have made them a treasured guardian. The sounds these pūpū harakeke made as they hastily retreated into their shells when disturbed in the dark of night once alerted the people to an approaching invader and saved their lives. Nowadays the empty shells are blown like a kōauau to create a special song.

Pūpūrangi

In the great kauri forests of northern Aotearoa, what appears to be fairy music is made by pūpūrangi or kauri snails in the high branches of the trees turning the lip of their shell into the breeze and creating an eerie whistle. They also make a whistling sound when retreating into their shells. These 'fairy flutes' can also become a fascinating instrument when the empty shells are blown in a similar way to the kōauau. Other shells also sing when blown this way and a trip to the beach takes on a new dimension as you keep trying out shells to find one that sings for you.

Pūpū harakeke, or flax snails eat freshly fallen leaves, and shelter in flax rather than feed on it. They grow to around 90 mm long and, interestingly, the smaller white sub-fossil shell is much heavier than the slightly larger one found recently.

HINEMOKEMOKE

Ko te Pūtara	Hear the signal of the calling shell of Kiwa
Ko te Pūtātara	Hear the clarion call of the trumpet of Tāne
Ko te Pūmoana	Hark, it is the conch of Tangaroa
Ko te Potipoti	Do you hear the voice of the Gods?
Ko te Pūwharaureroa o Matakaoa.	Yes it is the signalling conch of Matakaoa.
Hinemokemoke	How forlorn and lonely you are lovely lady.
Aue! Aue! Ai e!	
Mokemoke ana	How abandoned
Mokemoke ana	How lonely and separated
Tangi kau ana te hau	All that remains to be heard is the whispering winds
Ki runga te Maraenui o Hinemoana.	On the desolate Marae of Hinemoana.
Ko te Pūtara	
Ko te Pūtātara	The conch of Matakaoa thus calls
Ko te Pūmoana	Forlorn and lonely lady, Hinemokemoke
Ko te Potipoti	
Ko te Pūwharaureroa o Matakaoa	

Hinemokemoke e i! Hinemokemoke e i!
Aue! Taukiri e!

Hirini Melbourne^

Maureen Lander

Pūpūrangi, the giant kauri snail, is a carnivore which grows up to 75 mm long and can climb vertically.

5

Tāwhirimātea

The Wind Voices

Clem Mellish created this pounamu porotiti to resemble one described in old literature as having ears. It produces slightly different sounds on each rotation and, as its rotation changes, the stone gives out a small ringing note.

A group of porotiti showing how they can be created in a variety of shapes and materials.

Spinning porotiti

Tāwhirimātea, the God of the Winds, is usually acknowledged as a child of Rangi and Papa but sometimes as one of the wind children of Rangi and Pōharua te Pō. He and his family were some of those who opposed the separation of Rangi and Papa and, as we often observe, he and his wind children still do battle with the children of Tānemahuta, both plant and animal.

But the wind children are not always angry or mischievous and we appreciate them on a hot summer's day, or when out sailing and especially when we want them to chase the cloud children into hiding. It was they who went to the aid of Tānemahuta when he was attacked by the evil forces of Whiro as he climbed to the topmost heaven to collect the three baskets of knowledge so vital to human existence.

The very special sounds made by the winds as they whistle and moan or swish and brush against us are acknowledged as being messages from the Spirit World, for the wind people have no physical body. These spirit voices evoke strange feelings: we know we are hearing something special and we can learn to listen to them. Some instruments produce unexpected wind voices, and these are also considered special because they are perceived as spirit voices joining in with the song.

Porotiti

Porotiti, or humming discs, are usually oval discs with a cord looped through two off-centre holes. They are played by looping the cord around the hands, then twirling either cord or disc a little to start the spinning. By alternately applying pressure, then relaxing the cord each time it untwines, the disc will create its hum. Then, when the player blows gently on its vanes, it starts to sing and create its own songs. By varying the breath, new rhythms can be created. According to one informant, these instruments were named kōrorohū when they were just spinning, but kōrerohua when they were being blown on.

Although most living memories of them are as children's toys, porotiti are also used as song catchers: the player listens to the sound of the porotiti to set the pitch and rhythm for the composition of mōteatea or songs. They were also used as accompaniment to karakia or prayers.

Porotiti also create ultrasounds and vibrations and they were moved from finger to finger with fluid movements to ease arthritis pains and keep the joints flexible. When played over the faces and chests of sleeping children it was believed they helped to clear the mucus from their sinuses. They are one of several instruments that create quiet, private sounds and they can also become beautiful, functional pendants.

The porotiti in the illustration show variations created by following up an old written record of an instrument carved with 'ears'. Also included is a bird-shaped development that was suggested by these trials. The oval ones create more sound than the round ones but are a little harder to get started and must be well balanced. Those with holes or shapes cut into them sing louder, especially when blown on.

Porotiti can be made in a variety of shapes and from a variety of materials; even a strip of thick cardboard works well. Sometimes they were made from the circular discs that form the caps of whale vertebrae. The pilot whale or upokohue, which often strands on our shores, provides good-sized discs.

The rhythmic humming of porotiti as accompaniment to songs, such as the one that follows, adds an element of movement and a background of traditional sound which can complement the song in a strikingly powerful way.

A Soothing Porotiti Song

Tāirikiri taku porotiti	Whizzing
Tākumekume taku kōrorohū	Whirling
Pupuhi nei kia kōrerohua	Spinning disc
Taku kōrorohū	
Pupuhi nei kia kōrerohua	Blowing healing breath
Taku kōrorohū	
Pūrerireri taku porotiti	Soothing breath
Kōrerohua taku kōrorohū	keeping troubles
Wēwete nei I ngā kakatitangi	far away.
Ngā uauatanga o tēnei ao	
Hurihuri	
Takawiriwiri nei.	

Hirini Melbourne@

Pūrerehua

The pūrerehua, or rangorango is a bullroarer. Custom tells that the player's spirit travels up the cord to create the sound, which then travels on the winds to take the words and dreams of the player to the listeners of the world.

As part of the revival journey we have been taken to special sites by various local iwi to return the voices of Taonga Pūoro to the land. When we went to Onetahua or Farewell Spit, we were shown by the God of Winds, Tāwhirimātea, how he played the pūrerehua. As Hirini held his pūrerehua in front of him the strong

Terry O'Connor

This pūrerehua pounamu was made by Huata Holmes and named in the southern dialectal variant as **Hamumu ira gārara**. It is shown here lying on its korowai cloak made by Puti Rare.

Terry O'Connor

Rongopai is a whalebone pūrerehua with rows of manaia faces along its sides representing the people singing their message of peace. The surface carving represents Ngā Hau e Whā, the four winds.

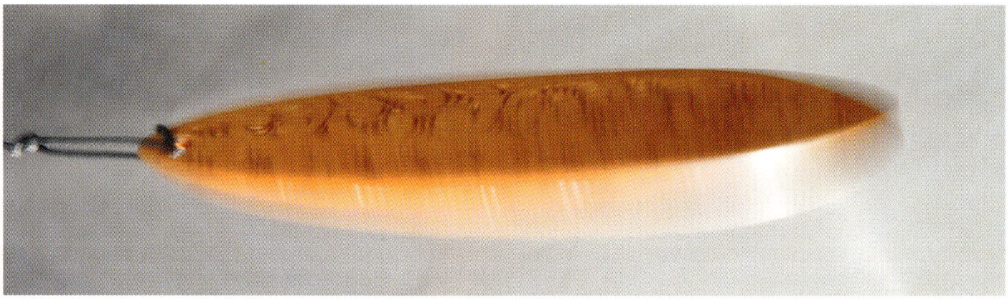

wind, which often lives there, took control of it and set it spinning. It soon had us awestruck as it sang its soul-stirring, whirling song in a way no human player could emulate.

There are many variations on the uses of these instruments. In Ngāti Porou some of these are famed as rain makers, causing tears of love to fall from the Sky Father, Rangi, on his beloved Papa, the Earth Mother. In Taranaki they are called mamae and sing a farewell to the dead. In the south they are named hamumu ira ngārara, which translates as the sound that stirs the lizards to life. When played, the sound would summon lizards from hiding, possibly because the vibrations simulate a blowfly's flight, suggesting food was at hand. A legendary pūrerehua pounamu played at dusk from One Tree Hill in Auckland was so powerful that it could be heard simultaneously in the Waitemata and the Manukau.

Pūrerehua are made of wood, stone and bone and in a range of sizes. The flight pattern, especially of the lighter and fatter wooden ones, resembles the moths from which they take one of their names. The other name, rangorango, belongs to a special blowfly that will fly, then hover, fly and hover. The pūrerehua song is likened to the whirring of rangorango's wings, varying in pitch as it darts and hovers, while the appearance of its flight is likened to that of a moth. When we were filming Taonga Pūoro one wet day at Ōhaka Tapu, we witnessed a korimako or bellbird dive perilously close to a pūrerehua that was being recorded. Unfortunately this was not captured on film but the bird's reaction caused some extra excitement that reinforced the concept of the instrument's southern use in replicating insect sounds.

A Song of Peace for the Pūrerehua

Pūrere rā te pūrerehua	Pūrerehua
Rewa rawa ki runga rā	Gliding
Ripia rā ngā hau e whā	Riding
Ruia rā te rongopai	on the Four Winds
Ruia te pai	To sow seeds of peace.
Ruia te pai.	

Hirini Melbourne* @ +

6

Raukatauri

GODDESS OF FLUTES

This old pūtōrino is one of the finest examples known and was collected by Captain Cook. It has been described as 'beautifully smooth and polished like the wood of an old violin'.[8] Collection of the Museum of New Zealand Te Papa Tongarewa (Ref. No. ME002502).

A casemoth seen beside the scarlet flowers of New Zealand's Christmas tree, the pohutukawa.

All the flutes of the Māori come down to us from Hine Raukatauri. She was a daughter of Tāne and she and her sister Raukatamea are the Goddesses of the Arts of Pleasure. Hine Raukatauri is best known as the Goddess of Flute Music. It is said that she loved her flute so much that she chose to live inside it. She is now personified as the plain-looking casemoth and the Māori make a unique flute in the shape of this insect's long case. The caterpillars of this unusual moth spin themselves a bag and camouflage it with tiny leaves, then hang from the branches in relative safety. Eventually the male caterpillars pupate and fly away, but the females remain within their hanging cases. In the quiet of night they cry for a lover and this sweet but barely audible sound is the touchstone for all Māori flute music.

When the demi-god Māui was seeking to gain control of fire for mankind, he had to trick his grandmother, Mahuika, into giving him all her fingernails which held the secret ability to make fire. When she threw the last fingernail into the trees to try to destroy Māui, he had to transform himself into a hawk to escape her wrath. This achieved his plan however as it put the potential for fire into the wood of the trees.

Before Māui could resume his human shape, however, he needed water to remove the sacred state of transformation. Naturally the birds he asked to help him were too afraid to do so, but eventually the normally shy kōkako brought the water. Māui rewarded the kōkako with several wishes and so this vain bird received its elegant looks and decorative wattles like the now extinct huia. But the kōkako had another request, to sing like Raukatauri, and so was told to eat the casemoths (a diet it still relishes to this day). The resulting sound of this songbird's pure notes and haunting calls has amplified the magical voice of Raukatauri, given us a touchstone for the songs of the flutes at a more audible volume and provided the reason for changing that minute sound into the louder songs of the various flutes.

Kōauau are the most common of the traditional flutes, of which it was once said that 'it was an amusement in every Pa to hear skilful players'.[9] The uses of kōauau were manifold. One of the oldest stories (see Chapter 7) tells of their use in entertainment as a group sought to unmask Kae by making him laugh. Many stories tell of lovers being won over by their sound, and of secret messages being sent through their song. The most famous story is of Tūtanekai and his friend Tiki playing their kōauau and pūtōrino on the island of Mokoia in the middle of Lake Rotorua. Their playing drew the beautiful Hinemoa in an epic swim across the lake to be with her lover, Tūtanekai. She was assisted by the ātahu, the vital and irresistible force contained in the message of the melody, but which also transcends both message and melody.

Native birds are known to interact with kōauau. I know of more than one occasion when a male bellbird, the korimako, flew down to within a metre of a nguru player, then fluffed his feathers and sang when the playing stopped. A duet ensued with the bird trying to fluff up larger and sing louder each time while several other korimako hopped around close by. On another occasion, in the forest of the Urewera, a kākā was called down and Hirini, Richard and I played several different flutes. After each one the kākā sang its own song, a different one each time. Finally, when one of us (unnamed, as is my prerogative as writer) played a nguru, the bird gave a very disgusted sounding squawk and flew off, leaving us quite enthralled but laughing at the unfortunate and unappreciated player.

All the flutes, however, had important functions beyond entertainment. They were used to welcome people into life and to usher their spirits out, to heal broken bones, to help memorise knowledge and as a medium for many special and very spiritual activities.

Kōauau

Kōauau are cross-blown flutes which were traditionally made from albatross wing bone, moa bone or human bone; a variety of soft and hard woods; and occasionally stone. A species of kelp, named kōauau, with its stem hollowed out, can also be played and was noted as a southern instrument. The sweetest sounds are those produced by kōauau made of human bone, but the mellow sound of soft wood, especially that of the neinei, has its own enchantment. However, it is the crisp purity of the ringing song of a stone kōauau that creates the closest replication of the bell-like notes of the kōkako.

Traditional kōauau range in length from a tiny wing bone less than 100 mm long, to a long wooden one of 385 mm. Most kōauau have three finger holes (wenewene) but occasionally up to five are seen. The smallest bone ones have no finger holes but a surprisingly large musical range.

According to legend, the patupaiarehe or fairies were the experts at playing the kōauau. As the sound travels far, an unseen player can still create drama in this way. Hirini was told by a crewman of a waka (canoe) that, when he and his companions were out on the river for early morning practice, they were spooked by the sound of a 'fairy flute' wafting through the mist. Hirini did not let on that he had been sitting on the riverbank composing a new song.

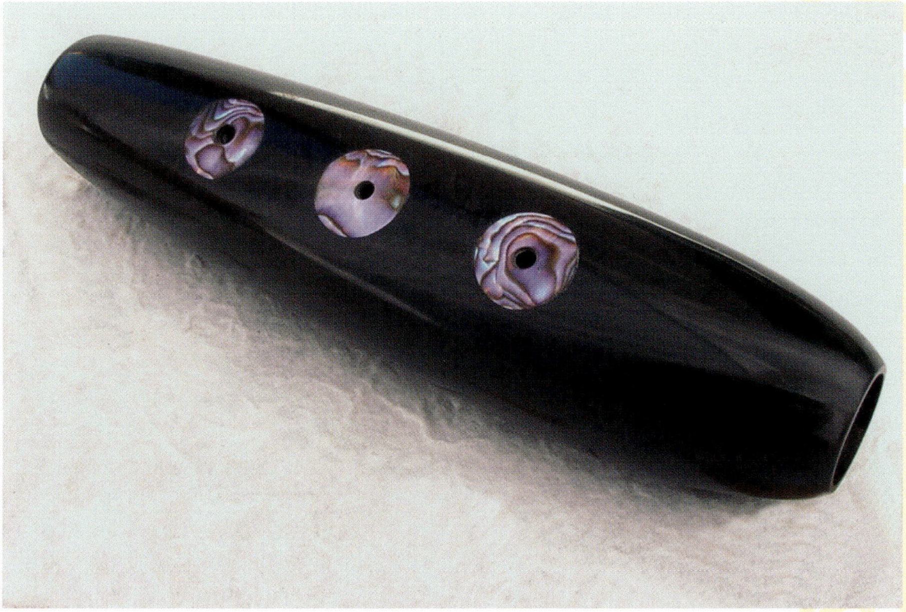

Tahu nui a Rangi, 'Southern Aurora'. A kōauau carved from argillite by Clem Mellish and inlaid with Rakiura paua shell.

Hirini Melbourne plays **Tangi Ariki**, his kōauau tōroa, a delicate sounding flute made of albatross wing bone.

A Kōauau Song About the Albatross

Tōroa tangi ariki	The tearful cry
E rere, e rere ki te rangi	The tears shed
Hai kawe atu i ngā roimata	of the Royal Albatross
Māturuturu roimata Tōroa	to adorn the chambers
Hai tukutuku mo tōku whare mokemoke.	of a broken heart.

Hirini Melbourne * @

Pōrutu

Pōrutu are essentially long kōauau with usually three (but up to six) finger holes of the same relative spacing as kōauau but located near the bottom end. They are capable of being over-blown to a second harmonic, and the ratio of bore to length has a critical bearing on this. I have often had to cut small amounts off before drilling the finger holes to create the dynamics of an easy-playing two harmonic flute.

Traditional pōrutu are recorded as being from 300 mm to 400 mm and up to 635 mm in length. The longest one had a bore diameter of 22 mm. Materials used were porokaiwhiria (pigeonwood), mataī and tutu. One, made from porokaiwhiria, was described as being between 300 mm and 400 mm long and 20 mm wide, and its aperture had been hollowed out with fire. The longest one was made from two pieces of mataī joined together. The bore had been finely honed by rubbing it along a stretched out cord that was kept charged with sand.[10]

The song of the pōrutu was much esteemed as being able to 'speak mouth words'. In one story a captured expert named Toheriri played it for several hours, so well that the meal was forgotten. In this recital he proved capable of playing a great range of music, first that stirred the captors to perform a haka, but then eventually a sleep-inducing lullaby. This enabled first his sweetheart and then Toheriri himself to escape.[11]

The lore of southern iwi places pōrutu among their principal flutes and the sound, which has a legendary carrying quality, was often ascribed to the māeroero or patupaiarehe, those seldom seen fairy folk.

Te Kaiwhakahaere, featuring Hirini, is a pōrutu carved from kanuka. It was begun several years previously, but was only completed after Hirini passed away.

Tiritiri o te Moana is a pōrutu carved from a chamois leg bone which has a natural beauty of line from any angle, giving this instrument a truly graceful presence.

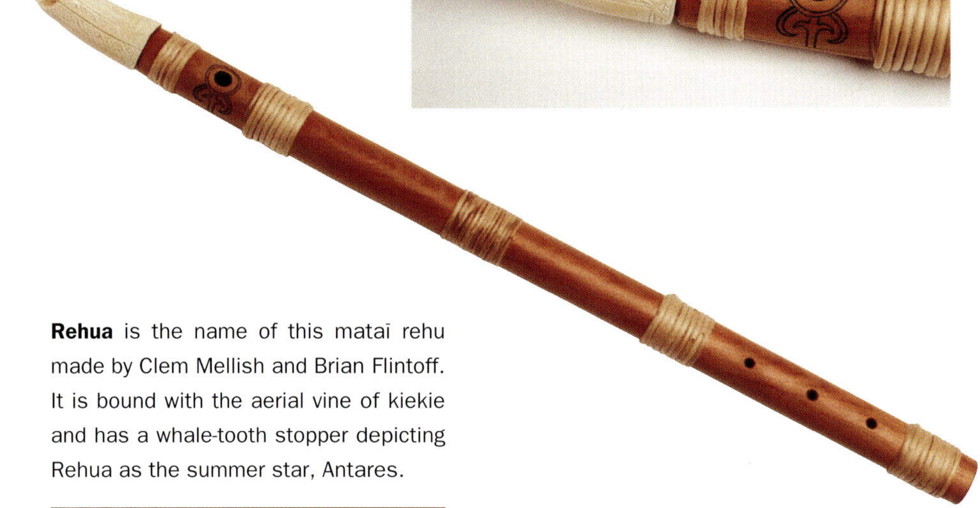

Rehua is the name of this mataī rehu made by Clem Mellish and Brian Flintoff. It is bound with the aerial vine of kiekie and has a whale-tooth stopper depicting Rehua as the summer star, Antares.

Terry O'Connor

Hirini Melbourne playing the first pūmotomoto replica made with two finger holes instead of one to test for the correct placement. Using the hole under his index finger he produced the sound remembered by his informants.

University of Waikato

Rehu

Rehu are long flutes with a closed top and a transverse blowing hole, but with finger holes like a pōrutu.Very few of these flutes have been recorded but the name is an old one with connotations that give a clue to it being a prized embellisher of song. Although the waha or mouth fipple is like a European flute, suggesting this could be a transitional instrument, the placement of finger holes (wenewene) as in the pōrutu creates a song with true traditional qualities.

Recorded examples vary from 345 mm to 570 mm in length and were made of mataī or tutu. A long description of an elaborately carved tutu rehu owned by a Canterbury settler says it was 570 mm long, had a 20 mm bore and was almost 40 mm at its widest point. The three finger holes, about 4–5 mm in diameter, were at 152 mm, 200 mm and 241 mm from the bottom end. Inside the bottom end and about 40 mm up was a constriction with a 4–5 mm hole in its centre. The top end was blocked with a plug after the pith had been removed. Another rehu was recorded as having no finger holes, the sound being modulated by partial covering the end hole.[12]

The contemporary example in the illustration is 460 mm long with a round bore around 18 mm in diameter. The top end is sealed and a slightly under-cut oval blowing hole of about 8–9 mm is fashioned about 40 mm from this end.

Pūmotomoto

Pūmotomoto are long flutes with a notched open top which becomes the blown edge and a single finger hole near the end. These are very special instruments whose history and indeed existence were only recently brought to life when Hirini talked with Tuhoe kaumātua from Waikaremoana. From that information I created a replica and Hirini returned some time later to play it to them. They verified that the sound was as they remembered and corrected details of construction.

The pūmotomoto is blown over a notch in the top while being chanted through and has only a single finger hole. It was traditionally played over the fontanelle of an infant in order to implant songs and information of tribal heritage directly into the child's subconscious.

Since the pūmotomoto needs to be about 575 mm long it is often easier to make it in two pieces and then join and bind them. A long branch of tutu or poroporo with the pith removed would also be suitable. The first tests used a gradual taper from about 25 mm at the waha (the blown mouth) down to 19 mm and this gave the sound remembered by the kaumātua. A single finger hole was located about 100 mm from the bottom. The mouth was shaped by sanding a flat surface at an angle. It is critical that this be very smooth and with a sharp, even cutting edge.

Nguru

Nguru are semi-closed cross-blown flutes unique to the Māori. Their enclosed bore gives a rounder sound than the kōauau and with four finger holes they have a slightly extended range.

Although nguru are popularly known as nose flutes they are more commonly played with the mouth, in the same way as kōauau. There has been considerable debate about the correctness of calling them nose flutes but sufficient tribal corroboration encouraged Richard to try playing them this way. We were sceptical about the results as the sound was less controlled and had extraneous wind noises caused by the blowing method. So he played the small nguru to Te Aue Davis, a kuia who is an expert in traditional songs. First he played an old song using his mouth and this drew an appreciative response. Then he played it with his nose and our expert began to cry. She later explained that, sweet though the mouth playing was, the nose playing and its extraneous sounds made her feel that she was with the ancients. She added that the ability of some nguru, in expert hands, to be nose flutes raises their status. The breath of the nose is more sacred, and those stray sounds created are perceived as the accompaniment of the spirit voices of the winds.

Nose playing is achieved by blocking one nostril with the right thumb and blowing through the other over the leading edge of the mouthpiece. Some nguru with larger end top holes can be reversed and played by the nose through that end hole, with the hand held over the instrument's large mouth.

Materials used for nguru are usually whale ivory, stone (generally soft stone like soapstone, limestone and sandstone), various woods, clay and the stems of gourds.

A Love Song for the Nguru

Ko te ngū	My breath
O taku ihu	of life
Mōhou, e te tau	is for you
Ko te tuki	My heart
O taku manawa	beats
Mōhou, e te tau	for you
Ko te roi	My eyes
O aku mata	ever look
Mōhou, e te tau.	for you.

Hirini Melbourne* @

Te Puna Waiora is a nguru made from a whale tooth. Carved underneath is a male moth with his wings depicted as enlarged hands.

Soapstone artefacts inspired this soapstone nguru carved by Bernard Makaore.

Pūtōrino

The pūtōrino is an instrument unique to the Māori and very highly esteemed. It has been called a bugle flute because it has two voices, but the traditional concept is of two complementary voices, the male and the female. Its male voice is played as a trumpet and its female voice as a flute. The shape of the instrument is taken from the casemoth cocoon that houses Raukatauri, Goddess of Flute Music, who loved her flute so much that she went to live in it.

The following legend tells why Raukatauri's flute has both female and male voices.

As dusk turned to night, and a dark night it was indeed, a moth flew by. He was searching for the source of a lonely, sobbing song that occasionally wafted on the still night air. The moth flapped his wings and flitted along seeking the spot where the love song appeared to have come from, but the alluring melody was elusive. He landed on the branch of a tarata (lemonwood) tree and looked around carefully, trying to spot the source of the sweetest song he had ever heard.

What caught his eye was a long bag hanging from a branch. It was wriggling and twitching. Then, slowly and gracefully, Hine Raukatauri emerged from her humble home. Her body was beautifully patterned with gracefully curving tattoos in yellow, white and black. Hine Raukatauri reached out for the diligent moth and they embraced, then joined their bodies in love. After their long embrace the moth was exhausted and was then taken into the cocoon by Hine Raukatauri. There he was consumed as nourishment for the eggs that would soon fill her home and become the new family.

The male trumpeting voice of the pūtōrino, its kōkiri, is a sound to summon or make people aware of something about to happen and each named call is given a meaning.

The female voice is usually played either in the same side-blown way as the kōauau flutes or blown over the top as in the photo of Hirini on page 19. It is sometimes a crying sound, and is used as such on appropriate occasions. From some instruments a third voice emerges, that of the mysterious Wheke, the daughter of Raukatauri, who is sometimes heard but never seen.

Although the pūtōrino has a limited range of sounds these can be varied to create a wide range of natural and enchanting effects that precisely convey the traditional voices. One recorded technique of a musician singing and playing at the same time on the pūtōrino is also used with the pūmotomoto. Some instruments can

Terry O'Connor

Mataī, with its noted acoustic properties, was used to fashion this pūtōrino named **Tūngoungou**, carved with the faces of Raukatauri and her lover Pepe.

Richard Nunns is blowing over one of the central mouths or kōkiri of **Te ara ki te Kainga**, a double pūtōrino carved by John Collins. This method creates a resonant sound effect rather like a hue puruhau.

University of Waikato

Terry O'Connor

These four very different pūtōrino show some of the variety in size and shape this type of instrument can take.

be played by blowing over the māngai or centre hole, and blocking the mouthpiece. Although there is no corroboration of this technique being used, it could also be perceived as the voice of that mysterious unseen daughter, Wheke.

For me, pūtōrino are the most special of all the singing treasures. I enjoy their individuality and look forward to completing each one I make to hear their subtle differences in sound. The uniqueness of their origins and construction, and their mystery, add to their appeal. But the range of emotions they can stir is their ultimate attribute. They depend greatly on the skills of the player who can elicit sounds ranging from the ghostly chill of an icy wind to the heart-warming resonance of a peace-giving hue puruhau.

Traditionally pūtōrino, which can vary in length from 227 mm to 655 mm, were made by splitting a length of mataī or other hardwood, shaping the inside and binding the two halves back in their original position. A sealant such as harakeke or tarata sap was applied, and held together by a vine binding of split aerial root of keikei, which, soaked and put on wet, shrinks to hold tightly on drying.

The end hole is usually only 2–3 mm, though a couple of examples, both from the Whanganui region, have a larger end hole that becomes the kōkiri or trumpeting male voice mouthpiece. Smaller pūtōrino have an inner shape that follows the exterior curve. These small instruments do not have the mature male voice of longer instruments, but they produce very clear, crisp flute sounds.

A few examples of double-chambered pūtōrino exist. These interesting rarities have an extended range and are much sought after. It has been observed that the sound flicking between the two sides is similar to part of the kōkako's song.

A Song About the Goddess of Flute Music

Te Pūtōrino a Raukatauri *Iri piri* *Runga peka e*	The Pūtōrino of Raukatauri hangs, clinging to its lofty branch
Kei roto ko te Puhi *O te tangi* *Korowhitawhita e*	Inside, a Goddess, Goddess of the music gives voice to loving song
He tangi hotuhotu, mokemoke *Mo te tau* *Kua wehe nei.*	A lonely song, A sighing song For her lover, flown away.

Hirini Melbourne*

Pūkāea

Pūkāea are long alphorn-like trumpets, which amplify the male sound of Raukatauri's flute. Although they are often referred to as war trumpets, pūkāea were also used to welcome people and to announce a variety of occasions, including the important ceremony of kumara planting. They were played to clear the path and ensure the well-being of the work of individuals, families and tribal groups. A stirring fanfare of several pūkāea was used to welcome in the new millennium at the dawn ceremony at Te Papa, which was relayed via satellite around the world.

Some instruments are capable of being blown over five or six harmonics, and will readily slide between these to create a spine-chilling sound. Pūkāea range from just 533 mm long to massive 2500 mm trumpets. One with a double bell is shown in some detail in Alexander Hamilton's *Māori Art.*[13] The cupped blown end or kōngutu leads to a bore starting at 5–12 mm, then gradually widening before belling out to the large mouth or whara. Near the whara end carved tonsil-like obstructions intrude into the bore.

A pūkāea substitute could be quickly made with spirally-wound harakeke (flax) leaves. These were named tetere and it was noted in 1864 that these were heard calling across an 'intervening valley sounding very sweet and clear'.[14]

A Path-clearing Song of the Pūkāea

Kōkirihia te Pūkāea
Hai whakaara i ngā karanga
O te whenua nei e,
Hai maioha i ngā reanga
Te ara mai nei e,
Hai waka kawenga
I ngā manako Māori.

Sound the voice of the Pūkāea
To draw forth the voices of this land
That they may speak to the new generations
Who will need to act
To realise the ambitions of Māori people.

Kōkirihia te pūkāea
Hai whakaara i ngā karanga
A ngā whaea e,
Hai whakahau i ngā reanga
Te ara mai nei e,
Hai pūmanawa
Mo ngā wawata Māori.

Sound the voice of the Pūkāea
To draw forth the voices of the mothers
To encourage the future generations
To be the agents of change
To effect the realisation of
the ambitions of the Māori people.

Hirini Melbourne*

John Collins carved this pūkāea, **Pōkai Whenua**, from a length of manuka tree which he carefully selected for its resonance. Its tone, range and volume show the wisdom of John's choice.

A detail of this pūkāea, **Whakamine Tānata**, carved by John Collins, shows the large amount of work put into trimming it to size and then later binding it with the vine, aka keikei. The research undertaken before its story evolved is one of the unseen attributes treasured by Ngai Tūhoe.

Terry O'Connor

7

Papa
THE RHYTHMS

The outside of these old poi are beautifully woven to shape around a central core. The mixture of plain and dyed dressed flax fibre or muka creates this striking tāniko pattern. From the collection of the Museum of New Zealand Te Papa Tongarewa (Ref. No. ME003940).

Several pahū have been made in recent years and it was a special experience for a group of us at a Ngā Puna Waihanga hui at Omaka Marae in 1995 to see one being partially carved with a tōki pākohe, or argillite stone adze. This tool was skilfully crafted by Dante Bonica on site from a rock taken from the river just days before. I had never expected to see a stone adze being made by the old processes, let alone being used, so the ancient sound made by that pahū imprinted itself on my memory for life.

Sometimes living variants of the pahū were made by cutting long 6–9 metre tongues on one side of hollow trees. These had a variable note depending on how far up they were struck. Some of these trees are still known by name and reputation.

Tōkere

Tōkere were castanets made of wood, bone, or a pair of bivalve shells. From an early description of them being played, with a pair held in each hand, the implication is that they were probably hinged in some way. Very little has been recorded of them but when we made a trial pair and showed them on a visit to Kahungunu kaumātua they were immediately and enthusiastically accepted by the late Ada Haig who performed a song with them.

An amusing illustration of just how new uses are found for unused traditions was relayed to us by an elderly woman who recalled tōkere made from the heavy end of the flax leaf. She said that they later made good clappers to chase the chooks out of the garden.

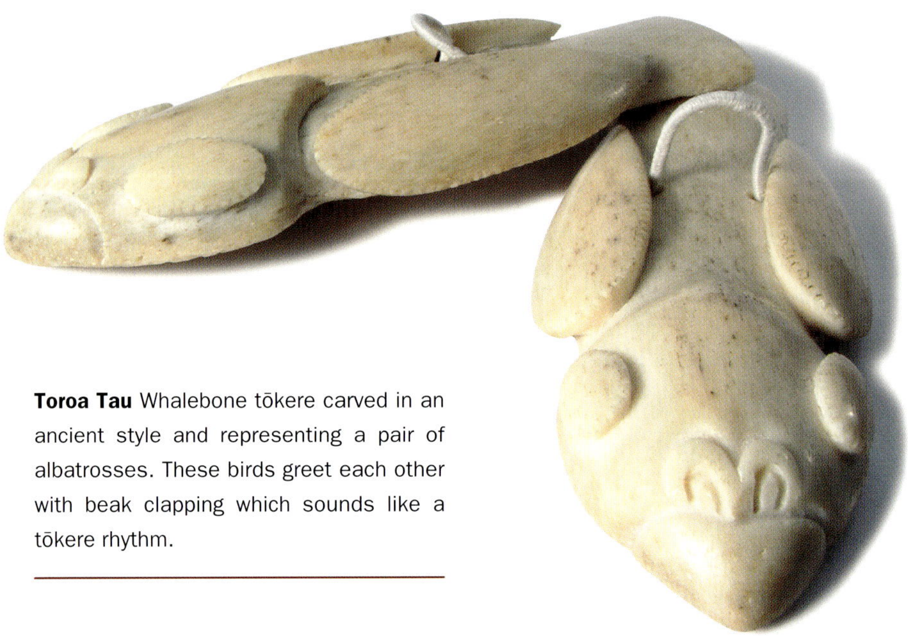

Toroa Tau Whalebone tōkere carved in an ancient style and representing a pair of albatrosses. These birds greet each other with beak clapping which sounds like a tōkere rhythm.

Poi • is an ancient dance form that comes under the tutelage of Hine te iwaiwa, the principal Goddess of Women's Arts. As the wife of Tinirau, she led the entertainment group that brought the wicked Kae back to face justice. Tinirau's sisters, Raukatauri and Raukatamea, who were specialists in their own fields of the entertainment arts, also feature here.

The great chief, Tinirau, called on the services of the famed tohunga, Kae, to perform the rites to bless his son. Afterwards Kae prevailed on Tinirau to lend him his pet whale Tutunui to ride back home on. Reluctantly Tinirau agreed but when Tutunui did not return and the faint but distinctively sweet smell of cooking whalemeat was noticed they knew what had happened.

In due time a plan was hatched to exact revenge for that terrible deed. In order to allay suspicions a party consisting of women only was sent as travelling entertainers. They had not met Kae but knew that he had broken teeth. So they set about making people laugh in order to find him without asking his identity. The troupe went from place to place until they arrived at Kae's village. Here they went through an extensive repertoire of singing, poi dancing, top spinning, mime with string games and puppets, and music performances that included the use of nearly all the instruments covered by this book. However the ever-suspicious and wily Kae kept a straight and unsmiling face until the lascivious words and gestures of a suggestive haka made him drop his guard, and in his laughing he showed his broken teeth with shreds of whalemeat still attached.

After all that everyone lay down and the women performed a special charm to put them into a deep sleep. They were not fooled by the paua circles Kae had placed on his eyelids to make it look as if he was awake. So, in the depths of the night they took the still sleeping Kae and paddled back home with him, where revenge was finally taken.

The most intricate rhythmic instruments of the Māori are the poi, balls that are swung on a cord and used to create stunning visual and sound effects. The sound of a group of poi slapping into hands in unison or hitting other body parts for a different effect is a truly stirring rhythmic experience. Along with the graceful movements and bodily gestures of the dancers, which are usually interpretations of the words of the chant, they create a uniquely expressive dance form. The

A pākuru made of black maire and its albatross wing bone striker. The pākuru was named **Rāpō** because the striker that suited it best was hollow and its opposite in colour.

Poi made by Dolly Gardiner-Paul from the swamp reed, raupō, with dressed flax or muka cords.

stamping of feet and the swishing of flax skirts or piupiu usually accompany poi and these create other uniquely Māori rhythms.

Different dances require different poi so there are ones with long cords of almost 2 metres and some with short cords of only 250 mm. Experts can swing four poi all moving differently at the same time.

The materials and the construction methods used in making poi affect the sounds they make on contact and the way they swing. Most old accounts describe poi as made from raupō or flax leaves and stuffed with the downy raupō seeds. Sometimes they were in a woven cover made with dressed and dyed flax fibre which created beautiful and intricate patterns. Their strings were made from plaited flax fibre and special poi were decorated with dog hair. Southern informants stated that the earliest poi had no strings and were thrown between rows of performers.[15]

Today's performers still use old methods to make poi for special occasions but often more durable or more colourful materials are substituted. Many performers prefer to make their own poi and so have them personalised to suit. Fortunately this tradition did not suffer the decline that other instruments went through and several books devoted to the subject, such as *The Rhythm and Life of Poi,*[16] have been published.

An Extract from a Poi Song

Ko te tangi o waku poi	The beat of my poi
Ko te patu o taku manawa	is like the beat of my heart
E ihi ake nei	brimming with excitement
Mai i te puna e	from the source
O te aroha	of love
Patupatu ana	So it beats!
Hotuhotu ana	So it sobs!
Taku manawa	My heart
Patupatu, pā	beating
Hotuhotu, hō	sobbing
E...i...e.	E...i...e.

From a song by Hirini Melbourne[17]

Pākuru

These were one of the instruments played to accompany a haka by the sisters of Tinirau when they went to find Kae, the killer of Tinirau's pet whale, Tūtunui.

Pākuru are long resonant rods held between the teeth and rhythmically tapped while being sung over. They are an intriguing instrument whose simplicity belies their performance intricacies, which are, as yet, not fully known. There are several descriptions of the player holding and tapping the pākuru while also dancing and singing. Sometimes a pākuru was just a springy rod of tanguru (tree daisy) or a similar resonant, flexible twig. This was held between the teeth and tensioned by bending, while being tapped as the player danced and 'breathed the words of a song or chorus upon the wood, causing the most pleasing vibrations or waves of sounds'.[18]

Other variations were more rigid, such as a 300–400 mm shaped and carved piece of mataī or porokaiwhiria (pigeonwood), flat on one side and convex on the other. This, too, was held between the teeth. The opening and closing of the lips while tapping with a hardwood rod, such as maire, created subtle variations of timbre in the accompanying rhythm.

Another pākuru was described as a carved rectangular bar about 450 mm long. 'It is held lightly between the fingers of one hand and struck with a small carved mallet while words are breathed on it.'[19]

Around 1870 Captain Gilbert Mair noted that pākuru were performed by 'a number of skilled performers, standing in a row, their swaying bodies and little tapping mallets keeping the most perfect unisons. Now rising shrill, or dying away in the mournful cadence of some love song, the effect is remarkably melodious and pleasing.' Other observations also mention it being played by a group and with 'young women joining in the chorus'.[20]

A rather different South Island instrument, also called a pākuru, was described as being made from a thick hollowed stem of tuturākau around 1 metre long and plugged at each end. It was more like a drum and was played either with a 600 mm wooden beater or a softer one made of aruhe (pigfern stalk), shark skin or whītau (rolled flax).

An Old Song for the Pākuru

Whakarongo mai taku hine,
Ki te tangi pai o taku pākuru.
Tāoro haere ana ki
Pari-kārangaranga,
Hei kawe atu i te aroha,
Rere tōmairangi i runga o te rau,
Tīorooro ana ki runga puke,
Hei waho i to moe,
E te hoa whakaipo e – i.

Listen now my lady love,
To my sweet-sounding pākuru,
Sending forth its melody,

In echoing cliffs resounding,
Breathing forth my love to you,
Sounding from hill and dale,
Arousing from sweet sleep
She who fills my nightly dreams.[21]

Tutunui, a southern pākuru made from a thick stem of tuturākau with its pithy centre hollowed out. The end is resealed with a carving of whale ivory. Beside it lies its beater of whītau, which is flax dressed in a way that keeps it quite stiff.

Terry O'Connor

8

Instructions
ON MAKING AND PLAYING

Though this pahū from Ngai Tūhoe appears to be a model, it is of great interest as it is the only one like it known to have survived. It is kept in the collection of the Museum of New Zealand Te Papa Tongarewa (Ref. No. ME000466).

Some of the instruments covered in this book are so simple to create that short notes have been included in the earlier chapters. For the more complicated instruments detailed notes are provided here. There is a separate section on making instruments with bamboo, as this has proved a practical substitute for use in beginners' groups.

Instruments covered in this section are wooden kōauau, bone kōauau, pōrutu, nguru, pūtōrino, pūkāea, pūtātara, porotiti and pūrerehua.

Playing Māori Flutes

Here are some tips on learning to play cross-blown Māori flutes.

1. Keep the finger holes covered as it is easier to begin with.

2. Set your lips and tongue for the lowest whistle you can make.

3. With the instrument at an angle to the lips and partially sealed against the outer side of the lips, move the kōauau into that jet of air.

There are two variables to master: the angle of the kōauau to the lips and how far towards the centre of the lips to hold it. So, with the kōauau toward the outer side of the lips and at quite an angle to the lips, slowly swivel it towards the centre while blowing. If this does not work bring it forward a little towards the centre of the lips and try again until the sound arrives, remembering step 2. (Basically you seal two-thirds of the mouthpiece against your lips and find the right angle to blow at. This is a bit to one side, just off straight ahead.) Soon you will be able to go straight to this position and excitingly you will find this new skill works on many things, like bottles or even some sea shells.

4. When you have mastered the basic sound, practise varying the pitch by making slight movements of your tongue and lips. This will create the flowing sound of these taonga, remembering that traditional music moves in microtones.

These steps give the basic techniques, but there are many aspects of refinement and other blowing techniques that take years to understand and master. Sometimes the player follows the melody or hints at it and at other times adds ornamentation. Breath vibrato and vocalisation while playing, together with fingering techniques and tonguing, will add more dimensions to the sounds made. Lessons are needed to advance to this level, along with careful listening to recordings. The DVD that accompanies *Te Hekenga ā Rangi* shows many of the instruments being played and it is a recommended resource for any student.

Hirini Melbourne playing a pōrutu made from the wing bone of a tōroa or albatross. These flutes are like a long kōauau with the finger holes near the lower end.

Terry O'Connor

These three kōauau are made from different materials, and show different ways of carving the end faces. On the left is a moa bone carved by Ranginui Keefe; in the centre one of rātā; and on the right an example made from the very hard maire.

Individualising Your Instrument

If you experiment beyond the measurements suggested above, you can create an instrument with a sound that suits a personal song or a required tone effect. Remember, this is a tradition in which each taonga is an individual with its own voice.

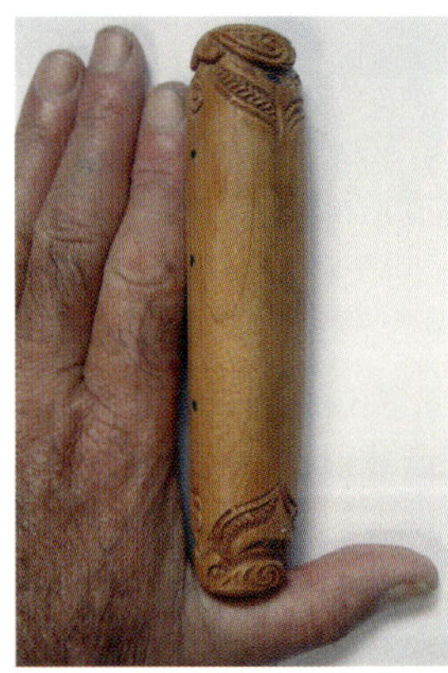

One recorded method of making a truly individualised instrument is to hold it as shown in the photograph (right) and mark the finger holes at the knuckle creases of your index finger. Leave a thumb width above the top finger hole. This method does not, however, suit some hand shapes and is not recommended for bone instruments, which do not have a tapered bore.

Making A Bone Kōauau

Because traditionally used bones are seldom available nowadays we often have to substitute other bone materials. Fortunately, sheep or goat leg bone gives a good replication of albatross wing bone; farmed emu or ostrich is just like moa; and lower leg bone from both the front and hind legs of deer is suitable to replicate human bone. I recently played both a very old human bone kōauau collected by Captain Cook and a contemporary one carved from emu bone and the sound was virtually identical.

The finger holes on **Te hā o Horohoro**, an ostrich bone kōauau, depict Māui Mua, Māui Roto and Māui Taha. This is one of the namings traditionally given to the finger holes. Another naming describes their function: te mea whakangāwari, the softener; te mea whakakaha, the strengthener; and te mea whakatika, the corrector.

Preparation

The shank bone is the one that has the required length and straightness. Here is one of several ways to prepare it.

1. Cut off the knuckles with a saw where the bone flares out, then boil the shank for 15–20 minutes to loosen the marrow and meat which can then be stripped off easily. (For small numbers this first boiling can be missed and the bone cleaned off manually or with a water blaster.)

2. Next, boil again for 10 minutes with a half-cup of liquid detergent to remove the oil in the bone. Then leave the bone in the sun to evaporate the water and oil. (If it was boiled first to remove the meat it will need a second boiling in detergent before drying.)

3. Any residual patches of oil can be removed by soaking overnight in white spirits (sold now as Fuelite), then evaporating the oil on a sunny windowsill or by the heat of a light bulb suspended about 100 mm above the bone.

There are several other methods that work well so seek advice if this seems too laborious.

Finishing

1. Cut the end off a bone where it flares out. It becomes thinner here and has honeycomb growth inside which must either be cut past or cleared out. Then cut it

to the length required. Generally this is between 100 mm and 120 mm for a sheep bone, and up to 180 mm or more with larger bones.

2. With a strip of 120 grit sandpaper pulled under the thumb of the other hand, round the ends of the kōauau to create a sharp but even edge on the inside.

3. Smooth off the bumps with the same sandpaper and method. Then, with 240 grit sandpaper, rub along the length of the bone to smooth it. A final rubbing with 400–600 grit, then burnishing it with another bone or rubbing with Brasso will make the instrument look really good. If you have a rotary polishing buff, Vonex or a similar polishing compound will give a great sheen to the bone.

4. Blow from the wider end, which usually has a peak to it. This blank produces your flute's lowest note and the pitch of the flute can be raised by shortening it.

5. Once you can confidently make your sounds, mark the finger holes. On a bone of around 120 mm the centre hole goes about the middle. The top hole is about 20 mm above this, and the lower one 25 mm below it. (Shorter bones may require only two holes.) The general pattern is that the distances between the finger holes get progessively longer from the first hole right through to the end. With the imperfections of a bone bore, the first hole must be closer to the centre than that of a wooden kōauau.

6. Drill holes with a 2 mm drill, then countersink slightly. (A suspension hole 5–10 mm from the bottom hole will not affect the sound, and will enable the kōauau to be worn.)

Kōauau from deer, emu and ostrich bones are usually made between 130 mm and 200 mm in length. On these longer ones the top and bottom finger holes can be moved correspondingly further from the centre one. Longer bones that will over-blow to a second pitch can also be used for pōrutu. (See instructions below.)

Bone is a great carving medium and carving a story on it will turn your instrument into a true taonga.

Pōrutu

I suggest you start by making an instrument about 250 mm long with a 15 mm bore drilled through it. This will create an instrument just like a longer kōauau with a different finger hole arrangement but similar acoustics. The spacing of the finger holes follows the general pattern of a kōauau with the distance between the holes increasing as you move down the instrument. For a 250 mm pōrutu drill the holes at 40 mm, 75 mm and 100 mm from the bottom end. Although all the old pōrutu I have seen have been simple, fairly plain tubes, a thicker, carved instrument will play just the same. Instruments observed and recorded have varied from about 250 mm up to 635 mm long, with bores from about 13 mm to 22 mm.

The long leg bones of ostrich and emu can also be made into pōrutu.

For the ostrich leg bone pōrutu in this illustration I added the carved figure of a personified Raukatauri on the end with her mouth open to sing through. This created back pressure which noticeably improved the dynamics of the instrument.

To create a long bore for these two pōrutu I made grooves in the two pieces with a router then glued them together.

Nguru

1. Cut a 100 mm length of 50 mm x 50 mm tawaī (beech) or other hardwood, Oamaru stone, Hinuera stone or soapstone.

2. Drill a 14–15 mm hole to a depth of 80 mm and smooth the bore with the reamer described in making a wooden kōauau.

3. Cut to shape as shown in the diagram then shape and smooth. The angle of taper at the mouth of nguru is noticeably flatter than for kōauau and pūtōrino and it is usually a defined surface rather than a rounded taper.

4. Drill 3 mm holes at about 22 mm and 45 mm from the mouth end and countersink these slightly.

5. Mark the bore depth on the side as an angle guide and drill a 4.5 mm hole from the upturn on the end to meet the bore.

6. Drill a 2.5 mm hole from the bottom end to meet the 4.5 mm hole as in the diagram, and countersink it slightly.

7. Sand, carve, oil and burnish as appropriate.

There are many variations in traditional nguru that have been measured, but we have found the smaller ones to be more suitable for playing with the nose. Usual materials are stone, whale ivory, the stem of a hue (gourd) and wood. If you are using wood, the very hard timbers like maire, pūriri or resinous heart mataī are the best. Wooden items tend to go quiet after they have been played for a while because condensation accumulates in the bore. A small poi muka or dressed flax tassel that fits into the bore of one old nguru suggests that it is a remedy for this. In his book, *He Nguru, He Kōauau,*[22] Mark Dashper gives details of making nguru and kōauau from clay. These instruments produce a clear ringing tone and I still have one given to me by Mark at our first hui at Te Araroa in 1985.

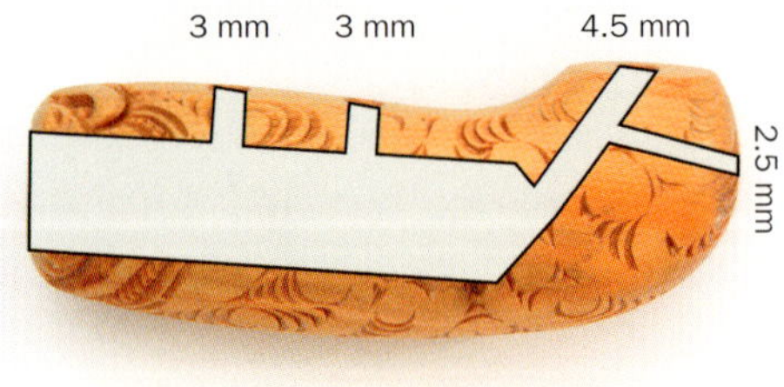

Cross-section of a typical nguru

Nguru vary in length from 72 mm to 160 mm. Bores range from 15 mm to 20 mm. Most have a slight taper, from 2 mm to 3 mm; a few taper the opposite way, becoming larger inside. There are between two and four finger holes on the main body. Sometimes the end hole enters straight into the bore but this creates a large variation in the pitch between the two end finger holes as opposed to the even pitch variations achieved with the model shown in the diagram.

Pūtōrino

The pūtōrino we have measured vary in length from 227 mm to 655 mm, with an average between 400 mm and 500 mm. The centre hole or māngai is most often at the mid-point and though usually oval (from 12 mm x 13 mm to 13 mm x 41 mm) it can be shaped to suit the carving and even have multiple piercings. This suggests that the opening is closed by cupping the hand over it rather than closing it with a finger. Occasionally a 5–6 mm hole is put directly beneath the māngai. The oval waha or mouth opening varies from 15 mm x 16 mm to 20 mm x 25 mm. The bore becomes more oval as it goes down, getting flatter by up to 5 mm but wider by as much as 13 mm. Most examples have a small outward bevel around the waha. Girth measurements at the centre vary from almost round (in double pūtōrino) to slightly oval (32 mm x 28 mm) or more oval (40 mm x 28 mm) and up to 70 mm x 30 mm. The end hole is usually only 2–3 mm, though for a Whanganui style instrument it may be a larger end hole which becomes the kōkiri, or trumpeting male voice mouthpiece.

It is to be hoped that someone will get the resources to view the interior shaping details of museum held examples which for now are mostly secret. As a general observation, the bore narrows vertically while it widens horizontally before opening to the sounding chamber which begins a little before the central māngai. In one of the few examples of an instrument that was in two halves and so could be observed properly, the bore in the top half tapered to nothing before the māngai. This would squeeze the sound down to the lower section then let it spiral up as it caverned out to the māngai. Initial experiments produce an exciting range of voices for this method (see illustration).

There does not appear to be any regularity with bindings, which vary from two to ten, with some almost covering the length either side of the māngai. Tests in practice show bindings improve the sound when the chamber walls are kept thin.

Making A Basic Small Pūtōrino

1. If splitting is not practicable and it is easier to get 50 mm x 25 mm timber, cut a 300 mm length of 50 mm x 25 mm mataī.

2. Mark the outline of the shape of a casemoth cocoon, keeping the waha or mouthpiece end about 30 mm wide, widening to 40 mm at the centre, then tapering to about 10 mm or 15 mm at the end. Shape the blank to this, then split it into two 40 mm x 12 mm pieces on a band saw. (Some carvers reverse the next processes. After the splitting stage they shape and carve the outside before creating the inner shapes as they have a better idea of wall thickness.)

3. Run a line about 4 mm in from the edge around both inner shells.

4. Draw a line across at 30 mm from the small, bottom end to mark the end of the sounding chamber.

5. Shape the insides of the two halves, taking special care to leave a smooth surface especially in the initial bore area where the sound is created. Scraping with a large washer, then burnishing by rubbing with a stone or even a teaspoon gives a good finish. If you are uneasy about the wall thickness a set of callipers can be easily adapted by adding inward pointing extensions, and you can write the thickness on the outside or on a paper template, as a guide for later shaping.

6. Apply a thin layer of epoxy glue, or other waterproof wood glue, to both halves, then seat together exactly so the saw marks fit back in place. Clamp the still solid small end and join, using very little pressure. (Thick rubber bands or spring clamps on the edges will usually suffice as clamp pressure in the centre will distort the thin walls.)

7. When set (it is best given 24 hours), tidy the exterior, taking care to get a smooth mouthpiece which tapers in to the bore. The reamer used to taper the bore of the kōauau is handy for smoothing the inside of the mouthpiece and removing surplus dry glue. Then shape, and smooth the outside to suit.

8. Drill two 9 mm holes side by side 150 mm from the waha, then join these to form the māngai, or central mouth. Curve the inner surface up towards the opening. A Dremmel cutter (the most widely used pendant drill in New Zealand) makes a neat job of this.

9. Drill a 3 mm hole from the small end into the sounding chamber. If this does not give an acceptable pitch difference when covered by the finger, enlarge the hole to suit.

10. You may drill a 5 mm hole directly below the māngai as was done to a few old examples of pūtōrino.

11. Sand smooth, or carve, then oil with linseed or Danish oil inside and out and leave to dry. (I tape over the openings and pour in oil to thoroughly season the interior.) Two dressings, a day apart, are normally sufficient.

Next day or when dry, burnish for a finishing sheen. Depending on usage, occasional re-oiling will enhance the performance of the instrument.

12. Bindings at each end of the pūtōrino and either side of the māngai can improve the sound. They are best inset to keep them in position. Fine cane has a similar tightening property to aka keikei, which is the best of the traditional bindings. Modern cords, such as fishing lines, especially ones with resilience, make an efficient substitute.

When binding start at the wider end. Thin the first 10 mm of the vine or cane where it will be under the binding, wind it all the way on tightly, pushing it close together as you go. Cut the spare off leaving about 200 mm to work with. About three or four turns from the end, hold the binding in place and loosen the last loops so that you can thread the end back under them. Then retighten those last loops one at a time and pull the binding tight before cutting it where it emerges. When

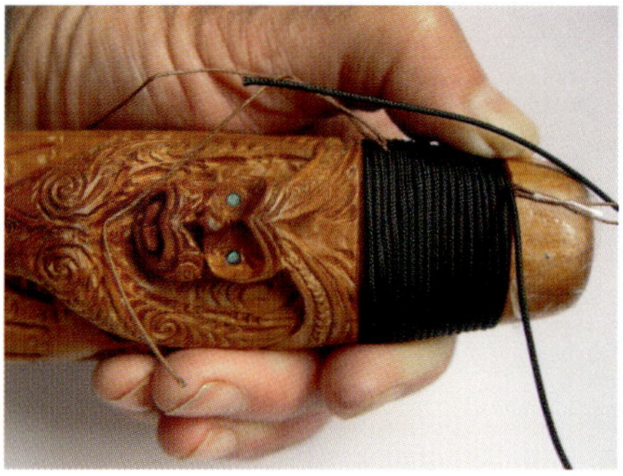

Māngai of the centre hole of an old pūtōrino with eight piercings.

doing the end bindings insert something in the hole to extend the instrument while loosening and retightening the cane.

If binding with cord, after the first five windings lay a loop of monofilament or strong linen thread to go under the binding. Use this loop to draw the spare end of the completed binding back under itself and trim where it emerges for a tidy finish.

Making a Long Pūtōrino with a Baffle

1. Shape and split as before, or use two pieces of 50 mm x 25 mm wood to give more depth for carving later. Shape the two pieces to match.

2. On the top section draw a line across 15 mm back from the centre māngai where the bore will be tapered to end (see photo).

3. Mark points 15 mm either side of the centre on this line, then points at 10 mm either side of the centre at the waha. Draw lines between these for the initial bore guides. Shape the sounding chamber as before following the curve of the instrument to about 40 mm from the end.

4. Begin carving out the sounding chamber on the other side of the line, rising sharply up to where the māngai will be opened.

5. Mark the bottom half to match the top, but carve out the bore groove evenly through to the sounding chamber.

6. Continue as for the smaller model.

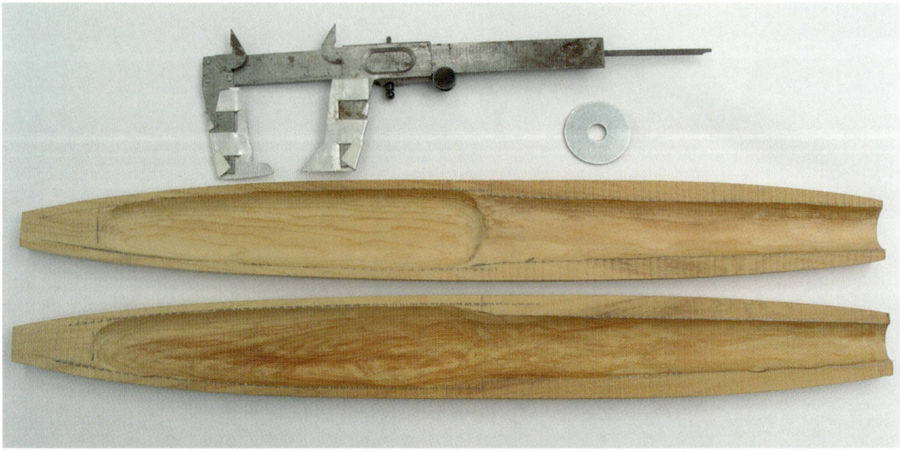

Beside this hollowed out pūtōrino blank is a washer which I use as a scraper, and a modified pair of callipers to check the wall thickness as a guide for carving the outside later.

Pūkāea

Pūkāea are made in two pieces then sealed and bound. Some old examples have a wrapping of material under the binding.

I have spoken to several makers who, in the tradition of individuality of the taonga, have successfully tried gradually widening bores, bores with a long straight section or with uneven gradations designed to add a waver to the voice.

Generally the preferred construction for an instrument with a controllable voice seems to be a gradually widening bore for about three-quarters of the length which then flares outwards. An old pūkāea in the Cambridge Museum, which is about 1800 mm long, is so narrow that it bows slightly when picked up. After many years of storage and silence it still has a clear, controlled range of voices.

The carved obstructions that intrude into the bore are usually near the whara, the large end, but one carver I spoke to prefers to include these further up the throat.

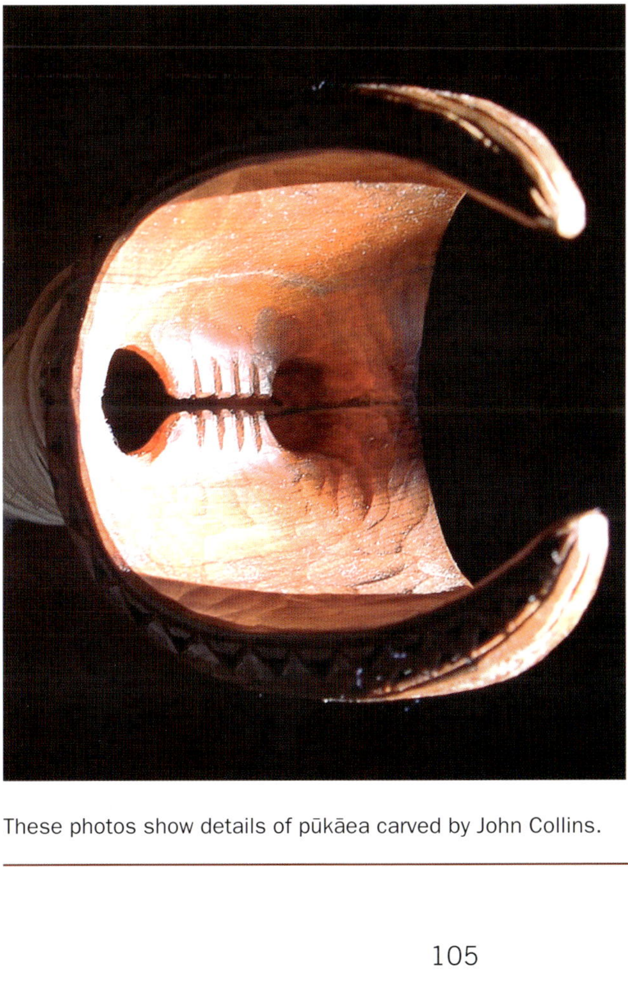
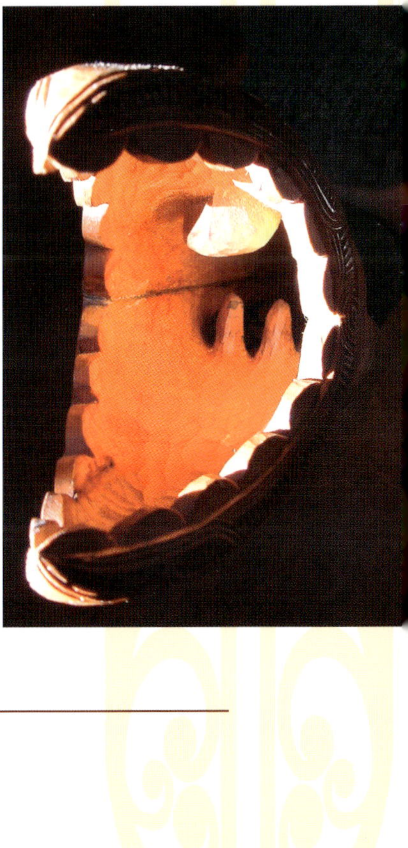

These photos show details of pūkāea carved by John Collins.

Making a Pūtātara

1. Using a diamond cutter or a tungsten carbide coping saw blade, cut the end off the shell to where you have an opening of about 10 mm. Check by blowing that there are no obstructions further down the spiral.

2. Smooth and tidy the shell opening and clear any blockage as tidily as possible with a diamond tool or a screwdriver. (Normally it will trumpet at this stage.)

3. Select a section of branch 100–150 mm long, or a piece of 50 mm x 50 mm mataī, tawaī or other hardwood.

4. Hollow the end of the mouthpiece to a depth of about 40–50 mm until you get a loose fit on the shell. The best way I have seen to line up the shell opening to the mouthpiece, is to tape over the end of the shell, smear some builder's fill into the hole, then push them together. Just before it sets hard remove the shell and it will leave an impression to guide your drilling.

5. Drill a hole of about 10 mm from this impression toward the centre front of the mouthpiece and another from the front to meet in the middle. I have tried several successful variations in the bore: a cupped mouthpiece like a brass instrument with 6 mm outlet, a 13 mm straight bore and a tapered bore from about 15 mm down to meet the large shell at 12 mm. Some with the wider bore can be blown like a kōauau so by creating a well-fitted impression and getting a good seal you can find the required sound with a few test blows before you fix the parts together.

6. When you are happy with the mouthpiece do the final shaping and carving. Then smear the sides of shell and mouthpiece with glue and push together into the first impression. (Knead-it, a mouldable putty, is great for getting an even fit from mouthpiece to shell ready for binding. It is also easier to get and to use than the kauri gum seen on old instuments.)

As aka keikei tightens on drying it is a good choice for binding. However joining shell and wood with pīngao (the ancient peace offering between the children of Tangaroa and Tāne) is also a good and appropriate choice. This can be secured by smearing with flax gum mixed with the red earth pigment, kōkōwai, which sets quite hard.

The smaller native shells are not always available and the larger triton shells are now scarce since they are listed as an endangered species. Other similar shells can be substituted and the photograph shows how a short-stemmed shell can be made to work by inserting the wooden mouthpiece into the shell.

Cambridge University

This well-worn pūtātara from the Cambridge University Museum was collected by Captain Cook's expedition to New Zealand.

Other shells can be substituted, and this photograph shows how a short-stemmed shell can be made to work by inserting a wooden mouthpiece into the shell.

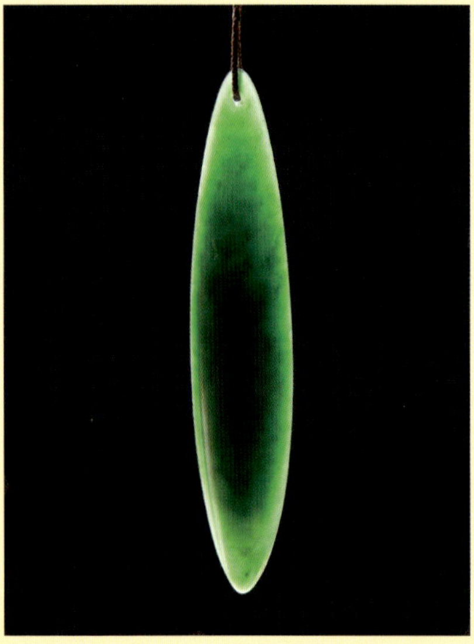

Porotiti are interesting instruments to make, as a variety of materials and shapes can be used to create slightly different sounds, especially when the porotiti is blown while spinning.

Na te Hukapō shows the beauty of pounamu as light penetrates its tapering edges. This special piece was created by Huata Holmes and blessed under the shadow of Aoraki/Mt Cook.

Porotiti

Porotiti can be made in a variety of shapes and sizes and from a variety of materials; even a strip of thick cardboard works well.

1. Measure the centre from either end and the sides then drill small holes 3 mm either side of the centre point on the long axis. With uneven shapes like the bird illustrated on page 56, the point of balance becomes the centre point.

2. A pliable cord is essential; thick cotton is enough for a card instrument. If you are having trouble and the discs seem reasonably balanced, the thickness of the cord could be the problem, so try a thinner one. Another common problem is caused by drilling the centre holes too far apart.

Cords of different lengths give different spin intervals. Start off with a cord about 1400 mm long as this can be doubled and the porotiti can also become a pendant. Drilling or cutting holes in the porotiti gives a new and louder sound. Making the edges on each side different will produce slightly different sounds on both rotations, as in the pounamu porotiti in the illustration, which has sharp and flat sides.

Pūrerehua

Crossways balance is important for pūrerehua though they can be less symmetrical lengthwise. They will start singing more easily if one side is flat or concave and the other side convex, but some surviving examples are of even thickness.

Length can vary to match the sound required. I have seen pūrerehua from 100 mm to over 400 mm long. A pair in a photograph in Hamilton's *Māori Art* are said to be 600–900 mm long.[23] The cords on these larger ones are attached to a long stick handle.

The wooden examples seen in museum collections usually have a long diamond shape. This gives a slower rotation and a less urgent sound, with a more erratic, moth-like flight pattern.

Remember that these are potentially dangerous missiles and must be on a strong cord, well tied and checked often. The pliability of the cord and the knot used can affect their playing so I do a double loop through the hole and tie with a bowline knot. I also add a toggle to the other end for both looks and safety.

To launch a pūrerehua, hold it by the edges between thumb and fingers with the cord stretched to the right hand above the head. As it is moved forward flick the thumb and fingers to start it spinning while applying power to the cord.

Making Instruments From Bamboo

Bamboo closely replicates the tutu and poroporo branches referred to in the traditions, but as it does not have their possible toxic properties it is an easily available and practical alternative. It is used for so many traditional flutes and other instruments in Polynesian cultures that in Hawaii it is esteemed as the 'singing tree'. Different sized sections can be quickly made into introductory versions of all of the types of flutes and also porotiti, southern pākuru and rōria. The flexible tip can be used to make pākuru and kū.

Making a Bamboo Kōauau

1. Select dead bamboo and cut into lengths of about 150 mm between the nodes. Bore diameters between 12 mm and 20 mm are recommended to begin with.

2. Cut strips of 120 grit sandpaper approximately 20 mm x 200 mm and round the ends. Select the larger end as the blowing end and be careful to get a sharp inside edge without curving into the straight cut.

We recommend learning the blowing technique at this stage as it is easier to do this without the finger holes.

3. Drill 2.5 mm holes at about 40 mm, 75 mm and 100 mm from the bottom end. (A 3 mm drill can be used for larger bores.) Countersink these to make them easier to locate with the fingers while playing.

4. Cleaning the bore of its papery lining with a round file will improve the instrument's sound and sanding the outside makes it look and feel better. A hole near the bottom end and on the other side to the finger holes will not affect the sound and will give a place to tie on a cord if you wish to wear it.

Making a Bamboo Pōrutu

With sections about 250 mm or longer, using the same hole measurements as for the kōauau above, you will create a pōrutu. This instrument has the exciting ability to be played in two octaves with slight alterations in the blowing technique. The length may need some fine tuning as the ratio of bore and length is critical to the ease of sounding the two ranges.

This collection of bamboo Taonga Pūoro includes; a kū, a pākuru, a pūtōrino, a pōrutu, a kōauau, a nguru, a karanga weka-karanga manu and a rōria.

Making a Bamboo Karanga Weka and Karanga Manu

Karanga weka and karanga manu can be made with the nodal section off cuts created when making the kōauau.

These can be used to craft double ended instruments as devised by Ranginui Keefe. A hole bored on an angle into the longer end makes that end into a karanga weka and the other end can be a karanga manu. Then trim to a length to create the required pitch and sand the ends round.

Making a Bamboo Pūtōrino

For a secondary school teachers' course Haumanu member Robin Slow devised a quick way to make a basic pūtōrino using a double section length of bamboo of about 20–25 mm diameter. Sometimes a single, very long section will suffice and this is even simpler to construct.

1. Cut just past the first node for a mouthpiece, then sand it smooth and rounded.

2. Drill two holes side by side just past the next node to make the centre mouth or māngai.

3. By using a long drill smaller than the bore to penetrate that next node, you will create back pressure similar to that of a carved instrument. If a Dremmel type drill is available it can be used through the māngai to cut and open that centre node.

4. Drill a 3–4 mm hole through the end node to complete construction.

5. Sand, carve, or decorate with a story, and oil to finish your instrument.

A Song to Start the New Day

Ka oho ake au *Te korihi a te manu* *Roto i te haeata* *Timatatanga o te rā*	I awake to the dawn chorus at the start of a new day.
Tiaho mārama e *Ki runga te whenua* *Te pūāwaitanga* *O nga hanganga katoa.*	The sun beams down bringing to life the flowering of creation.
Ka hangaia ano rā *He taonga kōrero* *Hei hōnore* *I ngā tūpuna e.*	I create anew A singing treasure to honour the ancestors.

This song was a koha to me from John Pou tū te Rangi Stirling, a gift which I now share with you.

9

Ki te Ao Mārama

Towards an Understanding of the Art Forms Used

Sir Tipene O'Regan asked me to carve this very large whale tooth which had long been a family treasure, or taonga. It contains elements of his Murihiku ancestral home, combined with family genealogy, and still retains the shape of the special tooth it was made from.

Taonga Pūoro must primarily be vessels that enable the creation of a particular type of sound. Their embellishment with carving does not usually improve the sound, but as each is created as an individual, the carving is an important addition, bestowing the respect that the instrument and its traditions deserves.

For those who wish to understand something of the art of the carved instruments that illustrate this book, I offer this brief summary of some aspects of Māori art. Like the rest of the book, it is but a glimpse into a special topic in this basket of knowledge. It is rather complex but that complexity defies further simplification.

Primarily Māori art is a conceptual art form where conveying an idea is more important than portraying a likeness.

Because it was an integral part of life, Māori had no traditional word for Art as we now know it. The basis of traditional art is illustrated in the purpose of the special fish hook that is still commonly worn as a pendant. Such decorative, non-functional hooks were lowered with the baited hooks in the belief that the Sea God, Tangaroa, who gave us the art of carving, would reward excellence of workmanship with a good catch.

Makohiku is an example of a stylised non-functional fish hook. It takes its name from the shape of its barb which copies the tail of a mako shark. The koru cut from the outer edge is a vestige of the notch or face carved on hooks to tie the bait to.

Right: In the large ira carving illustrated, the spiralling shapes represent the two ira, as do the two opposing cutout shapes. It demonstrates how the concept of ira is applied to art in many different ways to remind us to seek that same balance in life's many spheres.

If we examine this concept we see that because of the skills learned in making a special hook the functional hooks will be better, as will the lines, in order to keep the treasure safe. This striving for excellence would also have motivated the hook maker into developing other skills, and the combination of all these would ensure a good catch. That resulting good catch was attributed to the act of pleasing the Spirit World and so the rest of the community was inspired to do the same in their own spheres. Thus art elevated a people from the mundane to an ethic of excellence in a way which remains forever relevant.

The ethos of the design style of my carving is taken from Māori cosmogony, where creation began with the two complementary but opposite life forces coming together at Te Ahurewa, the Sacred Altar. Ever since, all creation has contained these two elements of Ira (life force) – Ira Atua (spirit) and Ira Tangata (physical). These are also seen as the male and female elements personified in Rangi and Papa. By keeping these in balance, harmony is created and maintained. Representing this balance with contrasting areas becomes the focus of design.

Carved by Clem Mellish, this pounamu tiki portrays a typically stylised human figure. If it is bisected, the concept that we are half spirit and half body is then represented visually .

A uniquely expressive and important Māori art element is named manaia. Its complex derivation is visible in the accompanying illustration. If a tiki, or human figure has its face and body bisected, then schematically it comprises the two elements of ira, spirit and body. When we isolate either half, the mouth has a characteristic beak-like shape with one eye and nostril in the head, and a body that takes on a sinuous look. This 'half body' form is the manaia. The word itself is a key to its significance as it embodies the mana, the prestige or power, of whatever it represents.

Here the half tiki has been rearranged. When put facing this manaia figure depicting a seal, it shows how the manaia concept can be perceived.

Individual parts of this manaia form can be used in isolation or rearranged to suit a particular purpose and the design area it must fit into. A manaia face alone is often used, either to represent some object or even concept, or to acknowledge a special attribute as a gift from the Spirit World. Often I use two rows of linked manaia faces along the body of a flute to represent the passing down of the twin traditions of words and tunes.

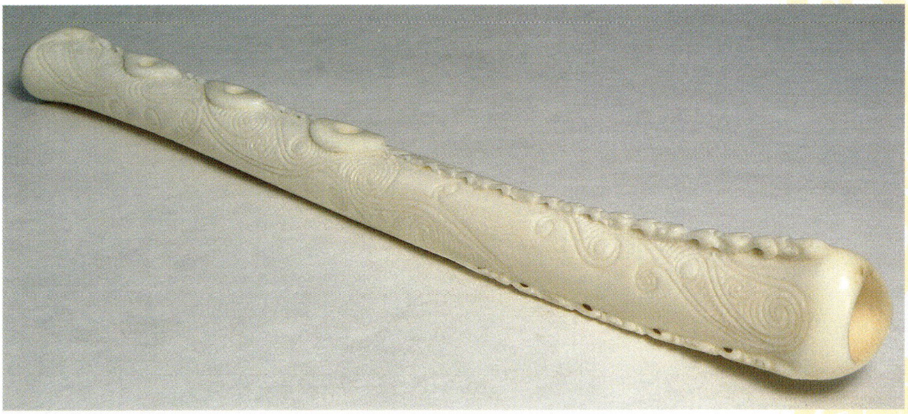

On this pōrutu two rows of manaia faces are shown representing the passing down of words and tunes. It is named **Tiritiri o te Moana**, which is an old name for the Southern Alps viewed from the Tasman Sea where they hover mirage-like above the waves.

Because in the Māori ethos a bird is perceived as a bird person, a tree as a tree person or a stone as a stone person, therefore the human-derived manaia spirit form can be ascribed to other beings also since they share the same spirit as people. However, the representation of other beings is not limited to the manaia form. Since a bird is perceived as a bird person, it is acceptable to carve it, or anything else, with the same stylisation used for a human person.

The manaia form sometimes takes a reverse twist as it has also developed to represent the physical aspect of any being. The conceptual nature of manaia is illustrated by the two examples below:

Paua

Fish

The paua is represented by a face only, as it resembles the shape of the paua, which of course has no legs. For the fish a curving body and hand has been added with the hand representing the fish's tail. In the carving on p. 118, the seal manaia shown opposite has a recognisable element to its stylisation with its forward curving flippers. However in the carving at the beginning of this chapter, the manaia faces at the ends of the whale's tail flukes are not in any way recognisable as they represent the spirit of the great albatrosses that glide gracefully across the Southern Oceans.

Although these uses of manaia allow the artist to tell a story in an excitingly unique way, the narrative must be known before the work can be understood, since a stone may look just like a person in spirit.

The kōkako carved on this pūmotomoto is depicted in similar form to a human with the enlarged hands representing his wings. His wattles are seen as koru on the sides of his lips, and a tail extends from the body.

Several traditional instruments feature a face on each end. We often carve a face on the blown end of a kōauau to represent the face of the instrument so that, when you are playing, you must bring the nose of the kōauau face to yours as in the traditional hongi or greeting. With the other end we can represent the face of the music. By giving this face two noses we convey the concept that the music is the combining of two breaths, that of the instrument and that of the player. Over the centuries other stylised conventions have been established that often bear little or no resemblance to their origins, and there is also a place for naturalistic depiction of all or part of a subject.

The surface of a carving is often textured with designs based on traditional patterns and these add to the story of the carving. The use of a Takarangi double spiral in surface designs reminds us of the complementary elements of Rangi and Papa and it usually indicates a point of movement such as a shoulder or elbow on a figure. On the lower set of this butterfly's wings, however, it depicts the typical eye of bright colour.

In this whale-tooth nguru, which is carved as a whale, the tail flukes of the whale become manaia spirit faces to acknowledge the great strength the tail has been given. The whale's face is carved in a traditional 'whale style' elaboration of the manaia face, but its pectoral fins resemble hands to show the mutual relationship between all life forms.

The two manaia faces which form the upper part of this butterfly's wings acknowledge the gift of flight.

Surface patterns may also be used as part of the story, as shown on the pūtōrino illustrated, where the pattern becomes the visual depiction of the unseen music creating its shapes in the silence. This pattern is also arranged in four design fields to represent the movement of these sounds out to Ngā Hau e Whā, the four winds, a traditional way of including distant people and places.

Chris Arnold-Kelly

The curled up koru is shown against the adult leaves which nurture it and feed its vigorous growth.

The most common shape in Māori Art is a stylisation of the curled up new fern frond called a koru. This conveys any of the many positive concepts that parallel the vigour with which the frond bursts into life.

To achieve the many aims of this art ethos, the artist must also be a skilled craftsperson; a medium; and a student of history, nature, myth, cosmogony and traditional lore. But when such artists work fluently in the Māori tradition, the powerful art forms that result can evoke responses which affect their owners and their viewers. It is no wonder that some carvings become famed icons, revered for generations and prized beyond price.

In this porotiti the koru is also shown as a cutout spirit shape. These shapes usually suggest further interpretation which creates an added dimension that can be personal to the owner. As well as a design element, they can double as a memory holder for a person, a special place or event.

Kōwhaiwhai

The use of koru is the main element in the traditional painted patterns, kōwhaiwhai, where the balancing of the complementary opposites is strongly portrayed in two ways. The white lines balance the dark areas and, in most traditional patterns, the red also balances the black. The shapes of all areas are carefully composed to be pleasing in themselves, and then the patterns tell a story.

Throughout this book individual kōwhaiwhai designs have been used to illustrate each chapter. Because the introduction and this Whakamārama have a similar explanatory role, both sections use a kōwhaiwhai design that incorporates the main elements of all the designs used for the other chapters.

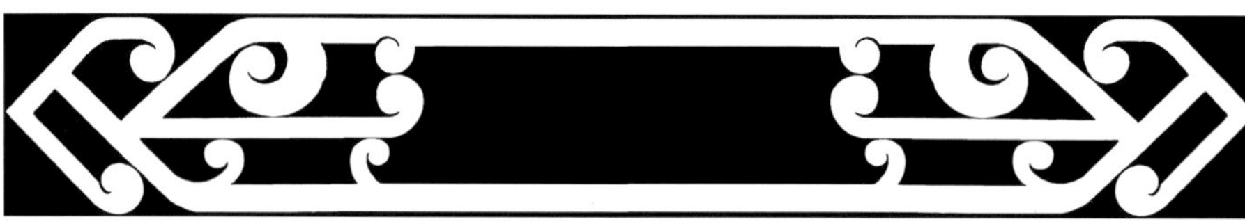

The simplified elements used for the design of the preface reflect its place as a starting section only.

For the design depicting the tunes of Rangi, the Sky Father, in chapter 1, the topmost element with its straight lines is doubled to represent the wind children. They are surrounded at each end by the rounder shapes of the cloud children. This design shows how the cloud children are constantly being chased around the sky by the mischievous wind children.

Chapter 2 on Hine pū te hue, uses the shape of the gourd with the music flowing from it.

Chapter 3 depicts Mataī, the tree used for many of the instruments. In this design we see the central straight trunk, the spreading limbs above and the roots below which are perceived as its hair. This upside down form was the only way Tāne could stop the trees and plants from moving around when he created them to clothe Papa after the separation.

The shells of Tangaroa are represented in chapter 4 by a pūtātara with its loud calls bellowing out from it.

The voices of the winds in chapter 5 use the wind pattern seen in both the sky design and in the designs showing the music flowing from the gourd and the shell. It is repeated four times in this design to represent Ngā Hau e whā, the 'Four Winds'.

In chapter 6 Raukatauri has a design which shows the spirit of Hirini's pūtōrino with its amokura feather resting between the two sides.

The design for Papa, the Earth Mother, in chapter 7 brings all the rounder design elements together.

Chapter 8 which gives instructions on making and playing the instruments uses the section of the design which depicts the body of the pūtōrino seen in the design for chapter 6.

Subtle rearrangements of the same elements make the differences between the design in the introduction and this one, used for chapter 9.

Mai i te Kakano

Mai i te kakano
Ka tipu he purapura
I ruia mai i Rangiātea.

Mai ngā pūtake
Ka ū mai te waiora
I ū mai i a Papatūanuku.

Mai ngā raureka
Ka ū mai te hauora
Ka ū mai i a Ranginui.

Ka puawai, ka pū ngā hae
Ka pua ngā hau
Ka kakano ano o tātou rā i tenei wā
Tīhei mauri ora.

From those Precious
Seeds of tradition
Planted in the ancestral homeland
of Rangiātea,
Nurtured by Mother Earth
and the Sky Father,
I take root, sprout leaves
Grow and flower,
To produce more seeds
and keep those gifts forever vital.

Hirini Melbourne#

Afterword

Throughout the journey that Hirini and I shared with these instruments, we had many connections through various bird feathers, especially the distinctive amokura feather. This comes from the tail of the red-tailed tropic bird, which was very special to the Māori who migrated here. When they discovered that the amokura does not live in Aotearoa it became even more precious. So I was overwhelmed when Hirini gave me a beautiful amokura tail feather, and even more humbled when I learned that it came from a bird brought here in a tropical storm. He explained that it was retrieved from a special pohutukawa tree where these birds are found distressed and dying after such storms. It can be interpreted that they give their lives to bring us these treasured feathers.

I knew it was hard for him to part with such a treasure so I finally devised a way to return it with honour by carving a double pūtōrino in which the feather rested between the two barrels – he is shown playing this instrument on page 19. Sadly, since he passed away, the feather has disappeared.

The instrument was made especially to hold that feather and remains therefore as a special bond between us. Now I liken the amokura that brought that feather here to Hirini's life, devoted to bringing us these singing treasures which he shared with all.

I discovered that one of the last songs Hirini had composed included the amokura; he had never recorded it. And just as Hirini looked at those pūtōrino in a museum all those years ago wondering what music they made, I wonder what music he sang to these words. I therefore thank him for the delightful stories that explain the origins of these instruments. I also treasure the memory of his tears when he told me of a recent student who had grown up listening to the singing of Taonga Pūoro and cried when she heard how she had nearly been deprived of that special part of her life.

This book is dedicated to all the coming generations who can now grow up with these treasures, but especially to Hirini and Jan Melbourne's mokopuna, Te Manukaimiro and Amokura – the loving lullaby that follows was written for Amokura. As with all the songs Hirini composed, only the words were ever written down and little Amokura is probably the only one who has heard it sung.

In the song presented in his own handwriting, Hirini likens Amokura to things most special to him rolled into one precious little bundle.

Illustration: Maggie Atkinson

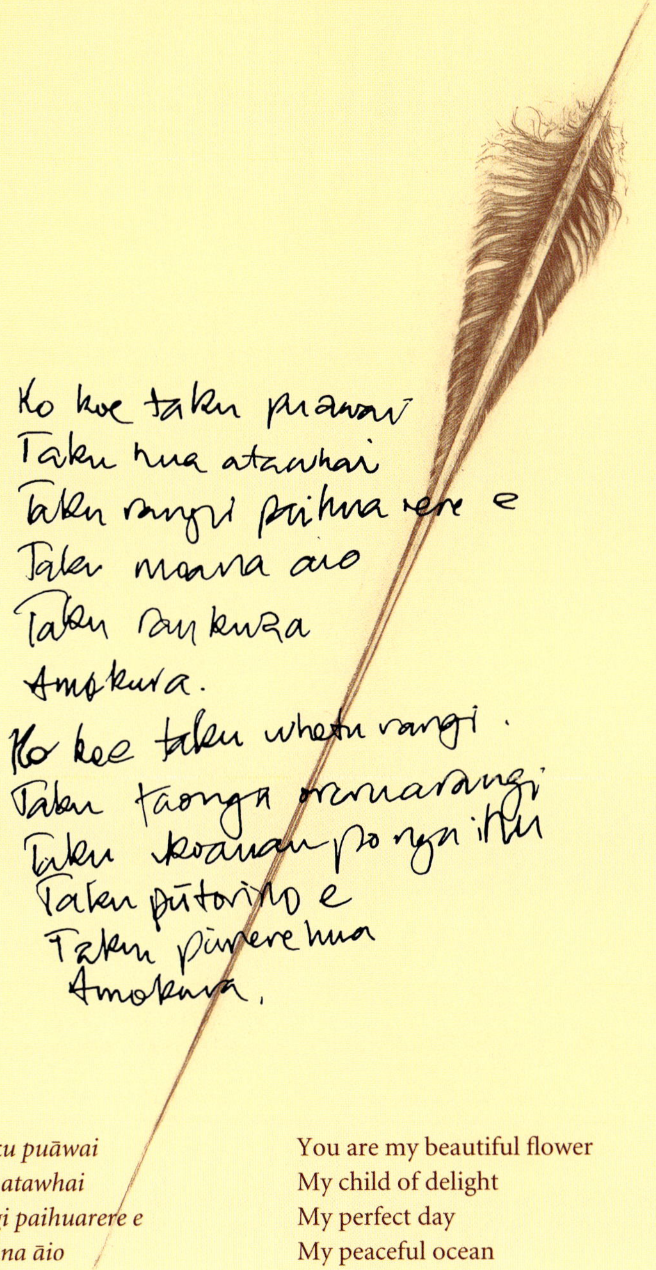

Ko koe taku puāwai
Taku hua atawhai
Taku rangi paihuarere e
Taku moana āio
Taku raukura
Amokura.

Ko koe taku wheturangi
Taku taonga ororuarangi
Taku kōauau pongaihu
Taku pūtōrino e
Taku pūrerehua
Amokura.

You are my beautiful flower
My child of delight
My perfect day
My peaceful ocean
My precious feather
Amokura.

You are the star in my sky
Like my ororuarangi you dance around
Like my kōauau pongaihu you soothe my soul
Like my pūtōrino special treasures you hold
Like my pūrerehua my songs you sing
My Amokura.

REFERENCES

1. Hirini Melbourne, Richard Nunns & Aroha Yates-Smith, *Te Hekenga ā Rangi*, CD and DVD, Rattle RAT DV010, 2003. **www.rattle.co.nz**

2. Melbourne, Nunns & Yates-Smith, *Te Hekenga ā Rangi.*

3. Johannes C. Andersen, *Māori Music with its Polynesian Background*, Memoirs of the Polynesian Society, Vol. 10, 1934.

4. *Traditional Music of the Māori*, CD, Viking VPS489.

5. *He Waiata Onamata, Songs from the Past*, Huia Publishers, 1998.

6. *Karanga Voices, Volume 4*, Asia Pacific Archive, School of Music, Victoria University, 2002.

7. National Wildlife Centre Trust, Pukaha, *Songs from the Forest*, 2002, National Wildlife Centre Trust, Mount Bruce, RD 1 Masterton. **www.mtbruce.doc.govt.nz**

8. Andersen, *Māori Music with its Polynesian Background.*

9. Andersen, *Māori Music with its Polynesian Background.*

10. Andersen, *Māori Music with its Polynesian Background.*

11. Andersen, *Māori Music with its Polynesian Background.*

12. Andersen, *Māori Music with its Polynesian Background.*

13. Alexander Hamilton, *Māori Art*, 1901, reprint Holland Press, London, 1977.

14. Andersen, *Māori Music with its Polynesian Background.*

15. J. Herries Beattie, *Traditional Lifeways of the Southern Māori*, edited by Atholl Anderson, University of Otago Press, Dunedin, 1994.

16. Ngāmoni Huata, *The Rhythm and Life of Poi*, HarperCollins, Auckland, 2000.

17. Huata, *Rhythm and Life of Poi.*

18. Andersen, *Māori Music with its Polynesian Background.*

19. Andersen, *Māori Music with its Polynesian Background.*

20. Andersen, *Māori Music with its Polynesian Background.*

21. Andersen, *Māori Music with its Polynesian Background.*

22. Mark Dashper, *He Nguru, He Kōauau*, Central Hawke's Bay Print, Waipukurau, 1996.

23. Hamilton, *Māori Art.*

SELECTED READING AND LISTENING SOURCES

Andersen, Johannes C., *Māori Life in Ao-tea*, Whitcombe & Tombs, Christchurch, 1907.
This contains a well-referenced collection of traditions.

Andersen, Johannes C., *Māori Music with its Polynesian Background*,
Memoirs of the Polynesian Society, Vol. 10, 1934.
Most of the information on instruments is contained in Part 6 of this volume.

Barrow, Dr Terence, *Traditional and Modern Music of the Māori*, Seven Seas, Wellington, 1965.
(Produced in connection with CD, *Traditional Music of the Māori*, Viking,
Seven Seas Ltd, Wellington, VPS489CD)

Beattie, J. Herries, *Traditional Lifeways of the Southern Māori*,
edited by Atholl Anderson, University of Otago Press, Dunedin, 1994.

Best, Elsdon, *Games and Pastimes of the Māori*, Dominion Museum Bulletin, 8, Government Printer,
Wellington, 1925, reprinted 1976.

Dashper, Mark, *He Nguru, He Kōauau*, Central Hawke's Bay Print, Waipukurau, 1996.
This small book contains making and playing instructions for kōauau and nguru.

Hamilton, Alexander, *Māori Art*, 1901, reprint Holland Press, London, 1977.
A large volume with illustrations, observations and notes on a variety of Māori artefacts

Huata, Ngāmoni, *The Rhythm and Life of Poi*, HarperCollins, Auckland, 2000.
Ngāmoni gives a glimpse into the many facets of the simple-looking but complex poi.

Karanga Voices, Volume 4, CD, Asia Pacific Archive, School of Music, Victoria University, 2002.
This recent CD recording has an interesting collection of bird and insect songs for those who find it hard to access and identify these sounds. These are supplemented by Richard Nunns's use of traditional ways to mimic the sounds.

McLean, Mervyn, *Māori Music*, Auckland University Press, Auckland, 1996.
Section 2, Music Ethnography, contains a wealth of information pertaining to Taonga Pūoro.

Melbourne, Hirini, *Toiapiapi*. (Book and accompanying tape.) Shearwater Associates Ltd, Wellington, 1991.
(PO Box 77, Paekakariki, phone (04) 905-7301, fax (04) 905-7302)
A preview is included of this soon to be released CD of the popular tape and booklet set, *Toiapiapi*. It features Hirini and Richard playing many of the songs composed by Hirini that are used to enrich these chapters.

Melbourne, Hirini, *Te Wharekura 41*, Learning Media Ltd, Wellington, 1994.
This booklet written in Māori by Hirini and its corresponding tape are now out of print but the booklet is available on line at **www.tki.org.nz/r/maori/wharekura/index_m.php** and the tape is reproduced, courtesy of Learning Media, on the sampler CD that accompanies this book.

Melbourne, Hirini, *Te Kuraroa*, CD, Kia Ata Mai Educational Trust, 1998.
Hirini, Kuini Beattie and Tama Renata sing a collection of Hirini's songs, including several used in this book.

Melbourne, H. & Nunns, R., *Te Kū Te Whe*, CD with notes, Rattle RAT-D004, 1994. **www.rattle.co.nz**
This very popular CD, which has been awarded a golden disc, is sampled on the CD that accompanies this book. It has shown the universal appeal of these ancient sounds, now made available to us just as the kōkako does by amplifying the secret sounds of Raukatauri.

Melbourne, H., Nunns R., & Yates-Smith A., *Te Hekenga ā Rangi*, CD and DVD, Rattle RAT DV010, 2003.
www.rattle.co.nz
The sampler CD with this book includes excerpts from this excellent second production from Rattle Records. This CD introduces some new sounds and adds the voice of Aroha Yates-Smith. Its theme is similar to this book in that it maps the creation story through the world of sound.

The accompanying DVD is an essential complement to this book for readers who wish to become players: it shows Hirini and Richard playing many of the instruments and gives further insight into the taonga and the process of creating music.

National Wildlife Centre Trust, *Pūkaha, Songs from the Forest*, 2002, National Wildlife Centre Trust, Mount Bruce, RD 1 Masterton, phone (06) 375-8004, **www.mtbruce.doc.govt.nz**
This delightful booklet and CD set maps the changing bird songs from dawn through to night, with accompanying notes and photographs. These are complemented by imitations of the huia's song and supporting songs by Rangitaane o Wairarapa. All proceeds go towards the restoration of Mount Bruce.

Songs from the Past, He Waiata Onamata, Huia Publishers, ISBN 0-908975-70-8, 1998.
A book and two-CD set of ancient songs with some instrumental accompaniment by Richard Nunns.

CD SAMPLER PLAYLIST

Track 1 **Pukaha; Songs from the forest.** www.mtbruce.doc.govt.nz
From track 4 'The night shift'. *00:30*
Ruru; the owls call.

Track 2 **Te Hekenga ā Rangi**. www.rattle.co.nz
From track 12 'E Taku Kuru Pounamu' *01:14*
Aroha Yates-Smith sings her farewell to Hirini Melbourne.
Richard Nunns plays his farewell on a pūkariri.

Track 3 **Te Hekenga ā Rangi.** From track 11 'Te Aho Kū.' *02:07*
Hirini Melbourne and Richard Nunns play kū and bow a guitar.
Hirini Melbourne and Aroha Yates-Smith sing.

Track 4 **Te Hekenga ā Rangi.** From track 6 'Te Auraki a Tāne' *00:34*
Hirini Melbourne and Richard Nunns play pūkaea, pūtatara and pūpakapaka.

Track 5 **Te Hekenga ā Rangi.** From track 8 'Hinemokemoke' *01:07*
Aroha Yates-Smith sings. Hirini Melbourne and Richard Nunns play pūtōrino and pūmotomoto.

Track 6 **Pukaha; Songs from the forest.** www.mtbruce.doc.govt.nz
From track 1,The Awakening. *00:32*
Kōkako and other birds.

Track 7 **Te Kū Te Whe.** www.rattle.co.nz
From track 4 'Hau' *00:54*
Hirini Melbourne sings. Richard Nunns plays a hue puruhau.

Track 8 **Te Kū Te Whe.** From track 5 'Koau' *00:35*
Richard Nunns plays kōauau ponga ihu.

Track 9 **Te Kū Te Whe.** From track 6 'Porotiti' *00:26*
Hirini Melbourne sings. Richard Nunns plays a porotiti.

Track 10 **Te Kū Te Whe.** From track 8 'Pūrerehua' *01:47*
Hirini Melbourne and Richard Nunns play pūrerehua. Hirini Melbourne sings.

Track 11 **Te Kū Te Whe.** From track 13 'Tangi mokemoke a Raureka' *00:47*
Hirini Melbourne plays pūtōrino, Richard Nunns plays kōauau.

Track 12 **Karanga Voices Vol. 4.** From track 32 'Choir cicada'. *00:22*
Cicadas sing.

Track 13 **Toiapiapi.** From track 5 'Toroa'. *01:28*
Hirini Melbourne plays guitar and sings. Richard Nunns plays a kōauau koiwi tōroa.

Track 14 **Toiapiapi.** From track 3 'Taku Pūtōrino'. *02:59*
Hirini Melbourne plays guitar and sings. Richard Nunns plays a pūtōrino koiwi tōroa.

Track 15 **Toiapiapi.** From track 16. 'Te Hau; Te Wai'. *02:27*
Hirini Melbourne plays guitar and sings. Richard Nunns plays hue puruwai and rōria.

Track 16 **Toiapiapi**. From track 8 'Te Nguru'. *01:16*
Hirini Melbourne plays guitar and sings. Richard Nunns plays nguru.

Track 17 **Pukaha, songs from the forest.** www.mtbruce.doc.govt.nz
From track 1 'The awakening'. *01:53*
Against a background from Pukaha of pipiwharauroa, kōkako and other birds singing,
John Stirling sings and plays guitar and kōauau.

Track 18 **Te wharekura 41.** Nga Taonga Pūoro Tawhito a te Māori. *47:00*
Hirini Melbourne reads the text and sings.
Hirini and Richard play a selection of instruments.

Track 19 **Karanga Voices Vol. 4.** From track 23 'Seabirds: diving petrel and shearwater'. *00:22*